Catherine H.Ch. Jackson

Old Paris

Its court and literary salons. Vol. 1

Catherine H.Ch. Jackson

Old Paris
Its court and literary salons. Vol. 1

ISBN/EAN: 9783337429225

Printed in Europe, USA, Canada, Australia, Japan

Cover: Foto ©ninafisch / pixelio.de

More available books at **www.hansebooks.com**

OLD PARIS

ITS COURT AND LITERARY SALONS

Volume I.

LADY JACKSON'S WORKS.

14 VOLUMES.

OLD PARIS. Its Court and Literary Salons. 2 vols.

THE OLD RÉGIME. Court, Salons and Theatres. 2 vols.

THE COURT OF FRANCE in the Sixteenth Century, 1514-1550. 2 vols.

THE LAST OF THE VALOIS, and Accession of Henry of Navarre, 1550-1589. 2 vols.

THE FIRST OF THE BOURBONS, 1589-1595. 2 vols.

THE FRENCH COURT AND SOCIETY. Reign of Louis XVI. and First Empire. 2 vols.

THE COURT OF THE TUILERIES, from the Restoration to the Flight of Louis Philippe. 2 vols.

JOSEPH KNIGHT COMPANY, Publishers,
BOSTON, MASS.

Anne of Austria

OLD PARIS

ITS COURT AND LITERARY SALONS

BY

CATHERINE CHARLOTTE, LADY JACKSON

"L'esprit de société est le partage naturel des Français; c'est un mérite et un plaisir dont les autres peuples ont senti le besoin."
VOLTAIRE

IN TWO VOLUMES

VOL. I.

With Illustrations

BOSTON
JOSEPH KNIGHT COMPANY
1895

Dedicated to

MRS. M. FRANKS

BY HER AFFECTIONATE FRIEND

CATHERINE CHARLOTTE JACKSON

IN REMEMBRANCE OF A PLEASANT RECONTRE, SOME YEARS AGO, IN THE GAY CITY OF PARIS

CONTENTS OF VOL. I.

	PAGE
INTRODUCTORY CHAPTER	1

CHAPTER II.

The 14th of May, 1610.—Coronation of Marie de Médicis. —Royal Procession at Saint Denis.—Coronation Fête.— Floral Decoration of Old Paris.—The Bourgeois King.— Popularity of Henry IV.—Henry in his Fifty-seventh Year.—Angélique Paulet.—The King's Coach.—Assassination of Henry IV.—Intense Grief of the People.—A Royal Widow's Weeds.—The Child-king Louis XIII.— The Queen-regent's Favourite 9

CHAPTER III.

Paris at the time of Henry IV.'s Death.—The Hôtel Saint Paul.—The New Louvre.—The Hôtel de Soissons.— Henry III.'s Vow.—Huguenot and Catholic.—Enlargement of the Tuileries.—L'Hôtel de Ville.—Le Pont Neuf. —La Samaritaine.—A Capucine Convent.—Saint Vincent de Paul 22

CHAPTER IV.

Statesmen and Generals.—Poets and Satirists.—Marie de Médicis.—The Poet Malherbe.—The Joys of Heaven.— Ogier de Gombauld.—Religious Novels.—"Astrée," a Pastoral Allegory.—Boileau's Opinion of "Astrée."—The lovelorn Marquis d'Urfé.—Diane de Châteaunormand.— A gentle Shepherd and Shepherdess.—Death of the Shepherd.—"Les Amours du Grand Alcandre" . . 32

CHAPTER V.

Betrothal of Catherine de Vivonne and the Count d'Angennes.—The Pisani Family.—The Nobles and Clergy.— Educated Women.—Marguérite de France.—Desire for Social Intercourse.—La Folie Rambouillet.—The Old Hôtel Pisani.—The Hôtel de Rambouillet.—The Salon

Bleu.—The Luxembourg Palace.—The Marquise de Rambouillet.—Rising Influence of Rambouillet.—The Marquis de Racan.—Armand du Plessis.—The Ladies of the Rambouillet Circle 44

CHAPTER VI.

Louis XIII.—The Brothers D'Albert.—Revels à l'Italienne.—Le Maréchal d'Ancre.—La Perle du Marais.—The Hôtel Lesdiguières.—The Cours de la Reine.—Statue of Henry IV.—Prevalence of Duelling.—The Queen a Peacemaker. — The Double Spanish Marriage. — Quadrilles d'Arioste.—Marriage Fêtes.—The Girl-queen, Anne of Austria.—Marguérite de France 58

CHAPTER VII.

Revolt of M. le Prince.—Elenora Galagaï.—Concini's great Wealth.—"The Accursed Jews."—Assassination of Concini. — His Wife burnt as a Sorceress.—The Queen-regent Exiled. — Armand du Plessis. — Marie's Return. — The Luxembourg.—Rubens' Twenty-four Paintings.—"The Day of Dupes."—Escape of Marie of Brussels.—Richelieu rules France.—Marie in Poverty and Exile . . 71

CHAPTER VIII.

Richelieu's Patronage of Literature.—Richelieu, Chapelain, and "Le Cid."—The Rambouillet Circle.—Its Discordant Elements.—Social Savoir-faire of the Marquise.—Depravity of the Court.—The Queen and Madame de Hautefort.—Richelieu and Anne of Austria.—Mademoiselle de La Fayette.—Louis XIII. as a Lover.—An Evening at Rambouillet.—The Fiery Calprenède.—"Le Grand Epistolier."—Cardinal de la Valette.—Eaves-dropping.—"Tel Maître, tel Valet."—Gaston d'Orléans . . . 83

CHAPTER IX.

Boisrobert.—M. le Prince.—The Mysterious Oublieuse.—Her Lute and her Song.—La Belle Angélique Paulet.—Her Music and Dancing.—The Jealous Nightingales.—A Presumptuous Bourgeois.—Patriotism, Religion, and Love.—A Noble Lover.—Galants et Honnêtes Hommes.—Social Supremacy of Woman 98

CHAPTER X.

The Urbanity Question.—Printed Discourses and News-Letters.—The *Mercure* and *Gazette de France.*—Romances of D'Urfé and Calprenède.—A Rival in the Field.—Madeleine de Scudéry.—Georges de Scudéry.—Julie d'Angennes.—Madeleine at Rambouillet.—Madeleine as a Poetess.—The Plays of Georges de Scudéry.—Georges a Virtuoso.—An Address to the Gentle Reader.—Success of "Le Prince Déguisé."—Georges popular at Rambouillet . 109

CHAPTER XI.

The Plague of 1631.—Terror of the People.—Wretched State of the City.—The Château de St. Germain.—A Royal Cook.—The Queen and her Ladies.—Anne and Louis at Thirty Years of Age.—The Rage for Dancing.—Richelieu's ostentatious Pomp.—The Regulation of Costume.—Mortification of the Noblesse.—The Right Divine.—The Plague at Rambouillet.—A Miracle . . 122

CHAPTER XII.

The Duc de Montausier's First Visit to Rambouillet.—Love at First Sight.—A Constant Lover.—Vincent Voiture.—His Sonnets and Letters.—His Letter to Madame de Sainctot.—Voiture *Réengendré*.—De Chavigny's Impromptu.—Voiture's Presumption.—Voiture in Love.—A Wager.—Two Sentinels.—A Privileged Buffoon . 134

CHAPTER XIII.

Conrart's Petite Académie.—The Cardinal's Secretary.—Admitted to the Salon Conrart.—Received as Tenth Member.—French Academy founded.—"Le Cid" of Corneille.—The Academy invited to decry it.—"Le Cid" first read in the Salon Bleu.—Le Dictionnaire de l'Académie.—Un Bureau d'Esprit.—The Vicomte de Combalet.—The Widowed Madame de Combalet.—Becomes la Duchesse d'Aiguillon.—The rival Salons.—The Salon Bleu still bears the Palm 145

CHAPTER XIV.

Contrasts and Changes in French Society.—The World and the Cloister.—Vincent a Popular Confessor.—He retires to the Oratoire.—Preceptor to the Sons of De Gondy.—Spiritual Director of Louis XIII.—Successful Appeals for Alms.—The Sisters of Charity.—L'Hôpital des Enfants Trouvés.—Le Commandeur de Sillery.—Story of Vincent's Earlier Life.—The Captive Greek.—Vincent a Friend to the Poor 158

CHAPTER XV.

Début of Mdlle. de Bourbon-Condé.—Her Toilette and her Cilice.—Her Desire to take the Veil.—Her Parents refuse their Consent.—Introduced at Rambouillet.—Armed against Satan's Assaults.—Anne of Austria.—The Cilice admonishes in Vain.—Anne de Bourbon converted.—The New Star and her Adorers.—The Château de Chantilly.—Its Gardens and Grounds.—Amusements of the Guests.—The Letter-Bag.—A Letter from Voiture.—Tossed in a Counterpane.—Marriage of Anne de Bourbon.—"The Cook's Daughter."—The Marquise de Sablé.—Beauty of Madame de Longueville.—An Attack of Small-pox . 169

CHAPTER XVI.

War with Spain.—Louis's Love of the Camp.—Birth of the Dauphin.—A second Enfant de France.—Le Grand Condé.—Marries Richelieu's Niece.—Morbid Fancies of Louis XIII.—Death of Marie de Médicis.—Sympathy of the People.—Richelieu's failing Health.—Cinq Mars.—Provokes the King's Anger.—His picturesque Appearance.—Un mauvais quart d'heure.—Death of the great Cardinal.—If a great Minister, but a poor Poet . . 187

CHAPTER XVII.

Louis once more is King.—Economy the Order of the Day.—Le Seigneur de Montauron.—Couverts à la Montauron.—Profuse Hospitality.—Corneille and his Patrons.—Death of Louis XIII.—Anne appointed Regent.—Paris at the Death of Louis XIII.—The Cardinal's Improvements.—Oases in the Desert.—Numerous Convents. . 201

CHAPTER XVIII.

Recovery of the Young Duchesse.—She reappears in the Beau Monde.—Chapelain's "Pucelle."—The Duchesse's Opinion.—La Guirlande de Julie.—Tallemant des Réaux.—Les "Historiettes."—Nicholas Rambouillet.—Madame de la Sablière.—La Haute Volée and the Financier.—Funeste Distraction 211

CHAPTER XIX.

La Bonne Régence.—Exiles recalled.—Captives set Free.—The Bishop of Beauvais.—The Duc de Beaufort.—Cardinal Mazarin.—His affected Humility.—Indolence of the Queen-regent.—Evenings at Court.—The Wily and "Beau

Cardinal."—Laurels and Bays.—Voiture, a Royal Favourite.—An Impromptu 221

CHAPTER XX.

War with Spain continued.—Rocroi, Thionville and Cirq.—Public Rejoicings and Fêtes.—Silly Practical Jokes.—The Young Hero and his Family.—Portrait of the Hero.—M. de Feuquières' Protégé.—An appropriate Text.—A Sermon at Rambouillet.—Début of a great Orator.—Un Charmant Homme.—A Fashionable Abbé.—The Abbé foresees a Rival.—The Abbé attempts a Sermon.—Interrupted by a Nervous Lady.—The Congregation disperses . . 231

CHAPTER XXI.

Old Paris.—A Leader of Fashion.—Reappears on the Cours. —Mdlle. Ninon de Lenclos.—Returns to the World.—Grief for the Loss of her Mother.—Representative Women.—Ninon's Accomplishments.—Soon Weary of Rambouillet.—The Salon of Ninon.—Theories of the Abbé Gedouyn.—The Court of the Marais.—The Queen's Order to Ninon.—A Pavilion at the Grands Chartreux.—A Lady of very high Merit.—Ninon strives to make a Convert 245

CHAPTER XXII.

The Convent of Val Profond.—The Abbey of Val de Grace. —Mansard's Original Design.—Education of the Young Princes.—Lamothe Le Vayer.—A Princely Education.—Two Terrible Turks.—The Duties of Piety.—The Royal Brothers.—The Court at Fontainebleau.—The Swedish Ambassador.—The Daughter of the "Ice-King."—Cartesian Philosophy.—The Ambassador Perplexed.—His troubled Spirit Soothed 259

CHAPTER XXIII.

Musical Art in its Infancy.—The Band of Les Mousquetaires. —A Promenade Concert.—Celebrities of the Court.—De la Rochefoucauld.—The French Navy.—Les Beaux Mousquetaires.—Le Comte de Coligny 273

CHAPTER XXIV.

The Mysterious Billets-Doux.—To Whom do they Belong?—Rival Belles.—A Tale of Turpitude.—The Lover and the Husband.—Public Apology Demanded.—Difficult Diplomacy.—A Doubtful Peace.—Dispersion of "Les Importants."—Coligny Challenges De Guise.—A Duel on the Place Royale.—Death of De Coligny.—"Argentan et Ismanie."—Triste Renown of the Duchess . . 280

CHAPTER XXV.

Preparation for the Public Fêtes Suspended.—A Defeat, a Victory and a Death.—Constancy Rewarded.—The "Carte du Pays de Tendre."—Woman's Social Equality Recognized.—Rambouillet on the Wane.—Claire Angélique d'Angennes.—A Duel by Torchlight.—Salons of Madame la Princesse.—Sévigné at Rambouillet . . 293

CHAPTER XXVI.

Victories of the Duc d'Enghien.—The Court Envious and Alarmed.—"Veni, Vidi, Vici."—The Duchess received by Turenne.—Her Conquests at Münster.—Death of Monsieur le Prince.—His Splendid Funeral.—Italian Opera Introduced.—The Queen's Piety Vexes Mazarin.—Mademoiselle de Montpensier.—Louis XIV. and Prince Charles.—The Rival Beauties Reappear.—La Belle des Belles Triumphant 301

LIST OF ILLUSTRATIONS.

Volume I.

	PAGE
ANNE OF AUSTRIA .	*Frontispiece*
HENRY IV. . .	32
PETER PAUL RUBENS . . .	78
CORNEILLE . . .	150
LOUIS XIII. .	188
BOSSUET .	238
DUKE DE LA ROCHEFOUCAULD	276
PRINCE DE CONDÉ (le grand Condé)	304

OLD PARIS

ITS COURT AND LITERARY SALONS

INTRODUCTORY CHAPTER

THE seventeenth century, in its literary and social aspects, is regarded by French writers generally as the most brilliant period in the history of their nation. It has been termed "the epoch of the true greatness of France," — "the true *Renaissance* of literature and *les beaux arts*."

It is indeed a period of very varied and romantic interest. Woman played an important part in it — contributing largely towards the reform then achieved in the French language, and in the corrupt and gross manners of the age, and introducing into the social relations of life that peculiar grace, fascinating ease, vivacity, and undefinable charm still vainly sought for in society out of France.

"*La vie de salon*," says M. Taine, "*n'est

parfaite qu'en France." And it is true. The social *réunions* of other nations have generally been formed on that model, and a more or less "frenchified" tone has been imported into them; yet the peculiar zest of that subtle, incommunicable essence of the brain, *l'esprit de société*, remains still, incontestably, the especial gift of the French. It is a part of the genius of the nation, and the language partakes of it; none other expressing with equal facility and felicity all that is lively, complimentary, witty, graceful, tender, refined.

From the time of Louis XII. — himself a liberal patron of learning, and in whose reign Greek was first taught in the schools of France — there had been occasional gleams of the approaching dawn of a fuller intellectual life. They were, however, but partial and fitful.

The young queen, Anne of Brittany, lively and *spirituelle*, learned, and accomplished for the age in which she lived, was the first royal consort of France who bestowed any appreciative patronage on literature, or sought to draw the wives and daughters of the nobles of the land from the seclusion and monotony of the *vie de château*, and to gather a social circle around her.

Those noble dames and damsels were willing enough, when it chanced that their feudal lords and masters consented, to lay aside their spinning-wheels and tapestry-frames at the bidding of their queen; and though very few, probably, could read either Latin or Greek with her, yet their presence enlivened the old Palais des Tournelles and the Château d'Amboise, and gave to the royal pastimes new spirit and variety. For this Bretonne Queen of France held a separate court, more splendid than the king's, and was attended by a more numerous retinue of courtiers, pages of honour, Breton guards, etc. She was reigning Duchess of Brittany, and, as such, exacted her full meed of homage, which Louis readily accorded her, being rather proud of "*sa Bretonne*," as he was accustomed to call this learned and rather self-willed royal lady. Jean Marot, the father of Clément, was attached to the court in the quality of her poet, and with the high-sounding title of "*Poète de la magnifique reine, Anne de Bretagne.*" *

Long years of Italian warfare, though most disastrous to France, enriched the royal library with valuable MSS., and the palaces with many treasures of art, the spoil of the wars; and Francis I. and some few of his nobles imbibed in Italy a taste for the *chefs-d'œuvre* of sculpture, painting, and architecture. Several of its most renowned artists were prevailed on to visit the French court, but none could be tempted to stay

---

* The splendidly illuminated *livre d'heures* of Anne of Brittany, preserved amongst the treasures of the Louvre, is a work of exquisite beauty and of the highest style of art.

there; though so great, we are told, was the veneration of Francis for learning and the arts, that when any distinguished *savants*, sculptors, or painters were presented to him, "he graciously made a point of advancing three steps to greet them."

But the Italian wars depopulated France; the heavy burdens laid on the people to exact the sums necessary for carrying them on impoverished it also. The lands lay untilled, the necessaries of life were scarcely obtainable, distress in the provinces was great and general. The uncleanly state of the then walled and comparatively small city of Paris caused frequent outbursts of fever, plague, and small-pox, which considerably thinned the population. The people were grossly ignorant, superstitious, and rough-mannered; and the court had degenerated since the days of the beneficent Louis XII. and his learned and virtuous queen,— it was without refinement; vice reigned there supreme. Immorality and obscenity, which passed current for wit and humour, were the chief characteristics of the writers then in vogue. The ladies of a literary bent composed "*devises d'amour*," as posies for rings and other jewels, or, when ambitious of higher flights, wrote licentious verses and tales, after the manner of those of Marguérite de Valois, the king's sister.*

* The lines attributed to the young widow of Francis II.— Mary, Queen of Scotland— when leaving France, are pretty:

Though Francis encouraged Italian artists, favoured *les belles lettres*, founded the College of France, began the rebuilding of the Louvre, and has left a name intimately associated with *souvenirs* of Fontainebleau, his reign was but a series of calamities, unfavourable to intellectual development and the amelioration of the condition of the people. He had devised measures for the increase of commerce and the improvement of the navigation of the Seine; but his wretched state of health, the religious dissensions, domestic disturbances, foreign foes, and impoverished exchequer prevented their realization.

Henry II. formed similar schemes; but his death, in 1559, from being wounded, accidentally, at a tournament, put an end to them. He had ordered the demolition of that unhealthy royal residence, the old Palais des Tournelles, and soon after his decease its walls were thrown down, and its pestiferous moats filled up. This fruitful cause of disease and death being removed

---

"Adieu, plaisant pays de France,
  O ma patrie,
  La plus chérie,
Qui a nourri ma jeune enfance!
Adieu, France, adieu mes beaux jours!
La nef qui déjoint mes amours,
N'aura de moi que la moitié;
Une part te reste, elle est tienne,
Je la fie à ton amitié
Pour que de l'autre il te souvienne."

from the too often plague-stricken city, the building of the palace of the Tuileries was begun in 1564. These and other works progressed but slowly amidst the crimes and bloodshed that were the principal events of the regency and reigns of Catherine de Médicis and her sons.

Charles IX., whose preceptor was Amyot, the translator of Plutarch, had an inclination for *les belles lettres*, and when prevented by weather from following his usual open-air sports would send for the poets to amuse him, and especially the poet *par excellence*—"*le prince des poètes*,"—the licentious, vain and intriguing Pierre de Ronsard. Charles even wrote a couplet himself now and then. But the influence of the queen-mother was fatal to her sons. Her crafty, bloodthirsty nature acted as a blight,—destroying every germ of good that appeared in them.

After the assassination of Henry III. the Leaguers, either bribed or worn by their sufferings during the siege into submission, opened the gates of Paris to Henry IV.; persecution then ceased, and after near forty years of civil warfare both Catholic and Huguenot were free to breathe in peace,—peace which the king believed he had permanently secured to the latter when he signed the edict of Nantes. A rough, but gay, gallant soldier, the greater part of whose life had been spent in the camp, and who when not making war was with the same persistent zeal making love, Henry was no great promoter of learning or liberal patron of the arts. He, however, very sensibly sent the royal library to Paris, as likely to be more useful in the capital than at the hunting-seat of Fontainebleau, whither Francis I. had transferred it from Blois, where Louis XII. had placed it at the suggestion of Anne of Brittany, since whose time it had been very greatly increased. Henry's especial taste was for building and repairing, and but for the restraining hand of Sully he, probably, would further have extended his works at St. Germain, Paris and Fontainebleau. He added a wing to the Tuileries, built the Pavillon de Flore, made some progress towards connecting the Palace with the Louvre, and carried out several improvements in Paris. He employed the poet, Malherbe, to write amatory verses and to extol the beauty of his mistresses. He could dash off pleasant stanzas himself, and very flattering *billets doux*, when inspired by the charms of the reigning *belle* of his too susceptible heart.

The example he set in his own mode of life was little calculated to reform the morals and manners of a dissolute court. But his tolerant spirit, his gay good-humour and apparent frank *bonhomie* in his relations towards his people, contrasted so favourably with the grinding tyranny to which, as if mere beasts of burden, they had been subjected by former rulers or oppressors of France, that they fully atoned in their eyes for all his excesses and shortcomings, which were indeed of a nature — such was the extreme grossness of the age — then generally deemed venial. His reign, though memorable in itself, was but as the first greyness of dawn to the flush of the opening day, the misty forerunner of an age of intellectual brilliancy and social refinement — "*le grand siècle littéraire*," which attained its climax towards the middle of the seventeenth century.

CHAPTER II.

The 14th of May, 1610. — Coronation of Marie de Médicis. — Royal Procession at Saint Denis. — Coronation Fête. — Floral Decoration of Old Paris. — The Bourgeois King. — Popularity of Henry IV. — Henry in his Fifty-seventh Year. — Angélique Paulet. — The King's Coach. — Assassination of Henry IV. — Intense Grief of the People. — A Royal Widow's Weeds. — The Child-king, Louis XIII. — The Queen-regent's Favourite.

IT was the 14th of May, 1610. Workmen to the number of eight hundred, or more, were employed in decorating the old city of Paris for a grand state pageant, arranged to take place on the 16th. Marie de Médicis, the second wife of Henry IV., was then to make her public entry into the capital, as the newly-crowned Queen of France. Her coronation, so long earnestly desired, so long delayed, she had prevailed on the king, after ten years of scolding and coaxing, threatening and entreating, to consent to. The cherished wish of her heart was obtained, and she had been crowned with the utmost pomp and solemnity, on the previous day, at St. Denis, by Cardinal Joyeuse.

Little or no sympathy or affection existed between Marie de Médicis and her husband.

His mistresses — less by their beauty than by gaiety and good-humour — held an influence over him which probably she herself might have acquired, could she have curbed her violent temper. But not only did she rave, and rage, and assail him with angry words, it was even sometimes necessary to restrain her from the too free use of her hands. And her blows were far from being light ones, for, as Henry once jestingly said, she was "terribly robust." From time to time whispers had reached her of the king's intention to seek a divorce, on the ground that a promise of marriage given in years gone by to the Marquise de Verneuil, invalidated any subsequent union contracted by him. Henry had not a very scrupulous conscience, but these whispered reports originated solely with the intriguing marquise. He entertained, at least, a kindly feeling towards Marie, notwithstanding her attacks upon him, and publicly paid her the respect due to the mother of the Dauphin of France.

But her brow had cleared since it had been graced by a crown. She was radiant with delight; for she had achieved a real triumph, — one especially gratifying to the feelings of a woman of her violent and vindictive character, — the Marquise de Verneuil, the king's mistress, and the Princesse Marguérite de France, his divorced wife, having both been compelled to witness that triumph and even to enhance it, by joining the train of ladies appointed by Henry to form her *cortége*. Her dark Italian eyes, which so often flashed with angry indignation on her faithless spouse, were then lighted up with a gleam of proud satisfaction that but few had observed in them before,— Henry, never.

The king had taken no part in the ceremony; he was present merely as a spectator. But when the royal procession passed up the nave of the old cathedral, preceded by archbishops and bishops in their richest vestments; the queen, surrounded by the noblest and fairest ladies of her court, and arrayed in splendid robes and sparkling gems, that well became her florid complexion and portly figure (she was in her thirty-seventh year), and wearing with dignity the royal mantle,— which, heavily embroidered in fleurs-de-lis of gold and pearls, was borne by pages of honour,— Henry, turning towards his minister and friend, De Sully, exclaimed in an animated tone: "*Ventre Saint Gris!*— *Qu'elle est belle!*"

This transitory revelation of beauty, due to the gratified feeling of the moment and the pomp and circumstance of royalty that surrounded her, took the king by surprise.

"I could throw myself at her feet," he continued, — after he had gazed long and steadfastly at her, and had replied to the proud glance she cast on him by a more amorous one than he had ever bestowed on her before, — "and worship her as a mistress, if I had not the misfortune to have her for a wife."

Henry was at that time preparing for war, and Marie, under the guidance of Sully, was to be regent in his absence. This was chiefly his reason for consenting to her coronation, and for the proposed great *éclat* to be given to her entry into Paris.

The narrow streets of the old city were more than usually thronged on that bright May morning. The Parisians were then, as now, a pleasure-loving people, and while many were busy with the preparations for the *fête*, many more were amusing themselves by looking on. Public *fêtes*, attended by any great pomp and parade of which the state defrayed the expense, were not numerous in Henry's reign. For the prudent Duc de Sully, who held the state's purse-strings, regarded all lavish expenditure of that kind as throwing money into the streets, and in one sense so it literally was. But on this occasion, the enthusiastic people supplied a bountiful tribute of floral decorations to mingle with and to add freshness and beauty to the tapestry and gold of the state and the banners and emblems of the various religious communities.

The fine *façades* of the new houses in the noble Place Royale and the Place Dauphine, then scarcely completed — though fashion had already sealed the former for her favourite abode, and both of which still remain the most interesting of the few *souvenirs* of the days of Henry IV. that modern Paris affords — were garlanded and festooned as if for a *fête* to the goddess of Spring. It was the season of flowers; and flowers and fruit, as an old writer tells us,* then grew in such abundance in the surrounding fields and gardens and orchards, that "they were to be had almost for nothing." In fact, from the Tour de Nesle, where the Institute now stands, to the Porte St. Victor; from the Place de Carrousel to the Porte St. Antoine; from the Porte du Temple to the Porte Marceau — the then extreme limits of Paris, north and south of the Seine — the manifold defects and desights of the old city were covered with a flower-gemmed mantle.

The object of all this enthusiasm was the king rather than the queen. The people delighted to honour him. They looked upon him almost as one of themselves; as a *bourgeois* king. The vicissitudes of his career had, indeed, often brought him into close companionship with many of the hardships and privations of humble life, and he was *rusé* enough to be able to turn this experience to good account. But at no time was there anything of the *bourgeois* in Henry IV.

* Sauval.

He had been a hardy, dashing leader of troops; gay and roistering, and without much dignity. When he unbuckled his sword, he cast aside for the time being all distinctions of rank, and sat down to be jovial and to enjoy himself with his comrades after the rough manner of the camp. But he was greatly changed since the days of "La belle Gabrielle." He had said that his heart had died with her, and that he could love no more. And perhaps it was true that he had never loved woman as he had loved her, though he had been more reckless and dissolute since her death, and to the crowning folly of his life was about to add its crowning scandal by entering upon a war that might desolate Europe for the sake of another Helen,— the young Princess de Condé, the wife of his nephew.

Yet no king of France, not even "*le père de son peuple*," the far more deserving Louis XII., had ever been so popular as Henry IV. His disposition was humane; he was cruel only where the preservation of game was in question; for that purpose his decrees were barbarous, for the chase was a passion with him when the excitement of war was wanting. Still, with all his popularity, faction was rife in the country and had never been wholly suppressed. Even then, as now, semi-barbarous as the people were, compared with their present intellectuality and general intelligence, they could never long endure peaceably and voluntarily the yoke of *any* ruler. And this effervescent spirit the feudal nobles, to a certain extent, encouraged, each being intent on maintaining his own independence.

This ever-present source of anxiety, together with other cares of state, domestic infelicity, and the irregularities of his life, had told greatly upon Henry, both physically and mentally, during the last few years. The gallant bearing, the sprightly jests that once distinguished "the ugliest, but bravest gentleman in France," were things of the past. Now, in his fifty-seventh year, his deeply-wrinkled face had become meagre and long; a careworn expression was almost habitual to it, and the once lively eye was sunken and lustreless. His shoulders were bowed, as with the heavy weight of years; his hair, once black and wavy, hung lank round his face, and, like his Huguenot beard, was bleached as with the snows of a wintry old age. His whole appearance was as of one who had been buffeted by the storms of life for the full span of the allotted threescore years and ten.

Notwithstanding these disadvantages, the king was then laying siege to the heart of Mademoiselle Angélique Paulet. And as he was always better pleased, rough soldier though he was, "by a conquest in love than a conquest in war, and from the universal homage he paid to woman still succeeded in pleasing the fair sex generally," it is probable that, had he lived, the new flame might have abated the ardour of the preceding one, and the meditated war have been abandoned.

On the morning of the 14th of May, Henry had visited the beautiful Angélique Paulet. She was the daughter of the state secretary who originated the tax, named after him, "La Paulette." The king, "*pour motiver sa visite,*" had with him his eldest son, the young duc, César de Vendôme, to introduce him to this fascinating young lady. She has been described as receiving her royal visitors "seated on a sofa of scarlet brocatelle, and wearing a morning-dress of blue silk. Part of her hair, which was of a deep golden colour, was twisted with a string of pearls and a blue riband, and part fell in long curls on her shoulders. The dress was made high, but open at the throat, displaying a necklace of diamonds set in gold, with a border of black enamel. Her sleeves were looped back with blue ribands, and her bracelets were of the same pattern as the necklace." This fair damsel, who was but seventeen, had won the admiration of the king by her graceful dancing and exquisite singing, in a "*ballet de la reine,*" danced by the court at the Louvre. Mademoiselle Angélique Paulet some years after was one of the celebrities of the Hôtel de Rambouillet.

Later in the day, the king had a fancy to see how the preparations for the 16th were progressing. He was accompanied in his coach by the Duc d'Épernon, and three or four other nobles. It was seldom he used a coach, owing, it has been said, to a superstitious presentiment of evil likely to befall him in one. But it seems scarcely necessary to assign superstition as his objection to using a coach, when we remember what sort of vehicles the Paris coachbuilders then produced. They were small open rooms (no glass windows),* either set without springs on a frame with four immensely large wheels, or suspended to long spokes by broad leathern bands. Thus, with a fair prospect of dislocation to the limbs of the occupant, these unwieldy constructions went jolting or swinging over the ups and downs formed by the mounds of dirt that impeded their progress in the wretchedly-paved and unpaved streets of the old city. And it required dexterous handling on the part of the driver to guide the four or six horses attached to these cumbrous conveyances, so as to avoid collisions in the narrow and tortuous thoroughfares. But, luckily, coaches were not yet numerous, and only

---

* Glass windows were not used until the time of Louis XIV., who sent a coach so furnished to England, as a present to Charles II.

the very rich could afford to take an airing in that stately and comfortless fashion.*

It was an unexpected obstruction by carts that afforded Ravaillac the opportunity of taking the king's life. Preparations for the *fête* had occasioned the employment of an unusual number of carts, and the royal equipage was brought to a standstill by two of them on that spot in the Rue St. Honoré (known to most persons who have visited Paris) which then formed the corner of the narrow Rue de la Ferronnérie. There, during the momentary confusion that ensued, the vile purpose of the assassin was but too fatally accomplished. He mounted the projecting steps of the coach, leaned far into it, and twice, with a dagger, furiously attacked the king; the second time piercing his heart.

Henry fell dead into the arms of the Duc d'Épernon. It was endeavoured temporarily to persuade the populace that the king, though wounded, was not dead,—but in vain; the fact of his assassination and the capture of the assassin spread rapidly through the city.

* Sauval (*Antiquités de Paris*) says that he had been told by a certain ancient dame — Madame Pilon — that there were no coaches in Paris until after the time of the League, some sixteen years before Henry's death, and that the first person to appear in one was a relative of her own, the daughter of an apothecary of the Rue St. Antoine, who had inherited a large fortune, and who was ambitious of distinguishing herself as a woman of fashion.

The chancellor, sitting in his apartment in the Louvre, hearing a great commotion amongst the soldiers on duty, called to the officer on guard:

"*Capitaine, qu'est-ce donc que ce fracas d'armes et de soldats de garde?*"

"*Monseigneur,*" replied the officer, in a tone of the deepest emotion, "*c'est que le roi est mort!*"

"*Mort! Ah! savez-vous ce que vous dites à? Et le chancelier lui pressa les mains, le regardant d'un air d'inquiète ménace.*"*

A wail of mad despair ran through the land—grief so intense that it became rage in its hopelessness. Yet, when the tragic death of the king was made known to the queen, she heard the sad news with exceeding calmness; though it had been revealed to her with fear, lest it should afflict her too deeply.

"*Elle ne parut,*" says Hénault, "*ni assez surprise ni assez affligée.*"

She seemed even elated with the thought that great power had fallen into her hands.

Sully and other friends of Henry IV. became suspicious of the queen, of the Duc d'Épernon, of Monsieur le Prince, and ventured to inquire of each other whether they who were to profit by this crime were not in fact its authors?

Henry was assassinated at about four in the afternoon. By six, the queen and the Duc d'Épernon had taken all the necessary steps to

* Vie MS. de Louis XIII.

secure the decree of the parliament declaring her regent. The ceremony of the previous day, by an extraordinary coincidence, had given her the right to claim it. On the 15th she appeared in the flowing black robes of a royal widow (as first worn in France by Anne of Brittany), with a veil of gauze taffetas reaching to her feet, and a full-plaited ruche of white gauze encircling her throat, the ends fastening in front like a scarf, with bows of black riband. Long Venetian sleeves, looped back, displayed the beauty of her arms, while the freshness of her complexion was becomingly subdued by the white ruche and the flowing gauze drapery of her veil.

Thus attired she proceeded to Les Augustines, where the parliament, on account of the expected *fête*, had assembled. She led by the hand the little king, Louis XIII., then eight years and a half old. He wore a violet velvet dress and a plumed hat of the same colour; thus giving much effect to the sombre but graceful robes of his mother. Her appearance made a great impression on the assembly, and it was generally acknowledged that she had never, even at her coronation, appeared to greater advantage. While speaking of the assassination of the king she excited sympathy by the abundance of her tears; and she is said to have been a woman of such violent emotions that the vehemence of her weeping was something startling.

The regency was conferred on her with full and absolute powers, also the guardianship of the young king, who, at her request, was required to give his *vivâ voce* approval in confirmation of the decree of the parliament.

The tragic manner of the death of Henry IV. had deeply impressed the child-king. This impression was deepened by the energetic words of his mother on this occasion, and the indignation and horror, the grief and resentment evinced by the parliament when referring to the wretched Ravaillac and his infamous deed. A dread of being assassinated took possession of the mind of the youthful Louis, and remained with him through life, rendering him suspicious and unjust, and often strangely affecting his conduct.

With the regency of Marie de Médicis began an entirely new order of things, both social and political. Italian favourites were in the ascendant. Concini, transformed into a Frenchman, as Le Maréchal d'Ancre, succeeded, without either experience or capability, to the important posts held for so many years by the Duc de Sully; and the millions of *livres* that prudent minister had amassed for the exigencies of the state passed into the prodigal hands of the queen-regent.

CHAPTER III.

Paris at the time of Henry IV.'s Death. — The Hôtel Saint Paul. — The New Louvre. — The Hôtel de Soissons. — Henry III.'s Vow. — Huguenot and Catholic. — Enlargement of the Tuileries. — L'Hôtel de Ville. — Le Pont Neuf. — La Samaritaine.—A Capucine Convent. — Saint Vincent de Paul.

PARIS at the time of Henry IV.'s death did not extend beyond the limits within which Charles V. had fortified it, about the middle of the fourteenth century, after having recovered the greater part of the dominions taken from his father, King John, by Edward III. and the Black Prince. These fortifications crossed the present Place de Carrousel, enclosing the old Louvre, built by Philippe Auguste as a royal residence in the early part of the thirteenth century. The Louvre was a feudal castle — the royal donjon-keep. It stood, until the time of Charles V., outside the city walls. Its deep moats were supplied from the Seine, and it was provided with every means that the military art of the day made needful for resistance and defence. Sauval gives full details of these repairs, additions, and embellishments of Charles V., by which the extent, the interest and importance of the Louvre appear to have been much increased.

John of France possessed a library of twenty volumes; his son increased it to nine hundred, placed it in "*La Tour de la Librairie*," and thus became the founder of the Bibliothèque Royale de France.

But while the old fortress of Philippe Auguste was undergoing repair, a less dreary abode was in course of construction for Charles. It was the Hôtel St. Paul, a perfect *maison de plaisance*. Its site is indicated by the present Rue and Quai St. Paul and Quai St. Martin. It had neither moat, battlement, nor arquebuse to defend it; the near neighbourhood of the Bastille being thought sufficient protection. The *grande salle* was a splendid apartment, with a finely-carved ceiling and painted walls. There were chapels and galleries, with painted glass windows, and numerous spacious apartments. On three sides extensive gardens and grounds surrounded it. They were planted with trees and shrubs, forming thickets and groves, with clumps of fruit-trees and patches of vegetables; park, orchard, kitchen and flower garden combined. There were dove-cots, fowl-houses, and fish-ponds; two fountains and a menagerie, and a pleasant green slope that led down to the river. Above all, there was a spacious court where tournaments and other sports took place.

Another royal dwelling, the Palais des Tournelles, turreted and fortified, became, after Charles V.'s death, the favourite abode of royalty. The Hôtel St. Paul fell to ruin; its gardens lay waste, and were afterwards built upon — such names as Rue de la Cerisaie, Beautreillis, Petit Parc, etc., being still existing traces of the ground they occupied. The old Louvre having suffered greatly in the wars with the English, its demolition was ordered by Francis I., who laid the first stone of the present magnificent edifice.

The new Louvre that was to occupy the site of the frowning old fortress was intended, as originally planned by Francis I., for a then modern and commodious royal dwelling. The works were but little advanced when Francis died, but they progressed so rapidly under Henry II. that his widow, Catherine de Médicis, on assuming the regency, left the unhealthy and already condemned Palais des Tournelles, and established her court at the Louvre. Its advancement was slow during the strife and bloodshed of the Médicis period; and besides, Catherine had determined on building a new palace contiguous to the Louvre, but outside the fortifications, on the vacant ground long used as *tuileries*, or brickfields. The architects she employed were Jean Bullant and Philibert Delorme, whose extensive design was carried out only as far as the *façade*. For during the erection of the Palace of the Tuileries, Catherine gave up the intention of residing there, and employed Bullant to build her another residence, which was afterwards known as L'Hôtel de Soissons, and on whose site now stands the *rotonde* of the Halle-au-blé with its surrounding streets. There, on the summit of Bullant's beautifully sculptured and lofty Doric column, — the sculpture defaced at the Revolution of '89, — Catherine and her astrologers studied the starry heavens and the course of the constellations, and sought to read in the movements of the celestial orbs a motive or excuse for the deeds of darkness and blood by which she desolated France.

The alterations or improvements that Paris had undergone during two centuries and a half had been made strictly within the walls, an inclination to spread beyond them in the time of Francis I. having been checked by a decree of the parliament interdicting the erection of any new houses in the faubourgs and the reparation of those falling to decay. Without some stringent measure of this sort it was feared that the provinces would be depopulated, and overgrown Paris became a *chef-lieu*, menacing in times of sedition to the rest of the kingdom, and capable of even bidding defiance to its sovereign; as indeed it did some fifty years later, at the time of the League. Then, Henry III., apostrophizing it as "*Chef du royaume, chef trop gros,*" vowed the vain vow, as he prepared to besiege it, that when subdued, he would so thoroughly raze it from the face of the earth that not one stone of its buildings should be left upon another to mark the spot where the rebellious city had stood.

As the population increased, new streets were made narrower, and the houses higher — the result of this crowding and huddling together being frequent outbreaks of sickness and pestilence. To escape from the impure air of the city was Catherine's motive for building a palace outside the walls. She had suffered greatly in her health at Les Tournelles, and the Louvre itself was then closely surrounded by squalid fever-stricken streets. The demolition of Les Tournelles was a real boon to the Parisians. It occupied with its walls, bastions, towers and ditches, a large tract of ground, which when cleared was disposed of, together with that covered by its extensive walled parks and gardens, by public sale. New streets, new churches, new bridges were planned; but beyond the planning little was done. The arts of peace could not flourish, for there was no repose in the country. The long struggle between Huguenot and Catholic had filled men's minds with murderous passions. Each one suspected his neighbour, and to be suspected of heresy was to have every man's hand against him.

Then came the League, with its incredible misery, sufferings and crimes. Catherine de Médicis dies, Henry III. is assassinated; but the end of the struggle is not yet. Throughout the land fanaticism raises her voice to heaven, and wildly shrieks, "Let France be saved from the greatest of all calamities, submission to a Huguenot king." But Henry is not deterred by trifles. "A kingdom," he declares, "is worth a Mass." Mass is said, and he is installed in his capital, and takes up his abode at the Louvre. Henry would have preferred the Tuileries, but found it too small conveniently to accommodate his court. The architect, Jacques Androuet Ducerceau, was, therefore, directed to furnish plans for the new wing and pavilion, and immediately to proceed with the further extension of the *grande galerie* of the Louvre — begun during the regency of Catherine. His purpose was to connect it with the palace of the Tuileries, for the king did not feel quite secure in his capital. And, according to Sauval, he was then very desirous of keeping open for himself a way of leaving Paris, in case of emergency, without being at the mercy of the populace, as his predecessor had been.

But as faction in a great degree ceased to

exist, and the religious fervour and religious hate of both Catholic and Huguenot calmed down, Henry IV. became a popular king. His wish (or the expression attributed to him) that every poor man had a fat capon to put in his weekly *pot-au-feu*, appears to have gratified the poor man almost as much as the gift of the capon itself would have done. "Smiling peace" was soon followed by plenty, for the lands around Paris, both to the north and the south, were so fertile, that with little culture (to quote Sauval again) they produced wheat in abundance, and all sorts of grain. Fruit was exceedingly plentiful, and "the vine grew and produced fruit luxuriantly, so that these lands might with reason be called the granary and the cellar of France." The improvements in Paris were numerous during Henry's reign. The arsenal was completed; the Hôtel de Ville also. Its western *façade*, arcades, and some other portions, formed part of the enlarged edifice destroyed by the Parisian populace during their last insane raid on the architectural glories of their city. The splendid staircase, some sculptured doors and ceilings, and the fine monumental chimney-pieces in the throne-room, still remained of the interior arrangements of the Hôtel de Ville of the time of Henry IV.

The Pont Neuf was also finished; it was then a very fine structure, with elaborately sculptured cornices, portions of which have been thought worthy of preservation in the Hôtel de Cluny. Spanning the Seine where the two arms of the river unite, the length of the bridge gave it an imposing appearance, and it was then the only one without houses. Half-way across it was erected the famous fountain, or pump, called "La Samaritaine." Two life-size figures in gilt bronze, of Christ and the woman of Samaria, sculptured by Germain Pilon, stood under a pavilion, and on either side of a large gilt basin, into which flowed a stream of water that was conveyed through a reservoir to the Louvre. On the top of the pavilion was a sun-dial, and, above that, a clock with chimes and small gilt figures, which struck the hours. The keeper, or guardian, of this edifice, bore the official title of "Gouverneur de la Samaritaine," and was allowed a good house close by for his residence. To keep the whole bright and in good working order, it was necessary frequently to regild the figures and repair the works. "The governor" was also an expensive personage, whose duties were performed by deputy. The Revolution of 1789 suppressed him; and, as in the case of more valuable mementoes of old Paris, the wretched mob greatly injured the ancient fountain, and defaced the figures of Christ and the Samaritan woman. Its machinery, its curious clock and famous chimes, were the work of Jean Lintlaer, a Flemish mechanician. The last vestiges of its ruined pavilion were removed from the bridge in 1803.

We hardly expect to hear of Henry IV. founding a convent, yet that of the severe order of Capucine nuns owed its foundation to him. He was stimulated to this act of piety, it has been supposed, by a priest sent by Pope Paul V. on a secret mission to the king, who was so much pleased with the papal envoy that he conferred frequently and privately with him. The priest, like the king, was a Gascon; *rusé*, and with the same disposition to banter, though of course more under control. Unfavourable rumours were then afloat respecting the sincerity of the king's adhesion to the Roman Catholic faith. His jovial air, and the little devotion his manner displayed when assisting at the services of the Church, had always kept doubt alive. But now he founds a convent of Capucine nuns! Some good souls thankfully accepted the act as a proof of their monarch's orthodoxy. To others it seemed more like a satire on his own mode of life; while not a few found a stumbling-block to their faith in him in his persistent retention of the Huguenot beard.

"If," they said, "it was a concession to the aggrieved feelings of his heretic subjects, it proved him to be but a lukewarm Catholic, or at least one who had not the courage of his convictions. The Huguenots, however, drew a hope from his continuance to wear it, that their renegade chief might yet be of the number of the predestined."

That he wore it from habit, or because he liked it, seems not to have occurred to either party. It was no doubt the cause of more than one of the many fanatical attempts to assassinate him, while a burning desire to avenge the dishonour his dissolute life had brought on some families instigated others. Whether the priest really suggested the convent, either in expiation of past misdeeds, or as a politic act at the time, cannot be confidently asserted. He was then an unknown priest, but in the following reign he exercised extraordinary influence in Paris, and many of its religious institutions and charities were due to him. He was a jocular, wily priest. He did much good, and some little harm, and used to say, laughingly: "*Que personne ne savait mieux remuer les écus dans les poches des riches.*" He was known then as M. Vincent — now, as a Saint, St. Vincent de Paul.

CHAPTER IV.

Statesmen and Generals. — Poets and Satirists. — Marie de Médicis. — The Poet Malherbe. — The Joys of Heaven. — Ogier de Gombauld. — Religious Novels. — "Astrée," a Pastoral Allegory. — Boileau's Opinion of "Astreé." — The lovelorn Marquis d'Urfé. — Diane de Châteaunormand. — A gentle Shepherd and Shepherdess. — Death of the Shepherd. — "Les Amours du Grand Alcandre."

MOST of the distinguished men who shed lustre on the reign of Louis XIV., whether as statesmen, generals, men of letters, poets, painters, etc., as well as the prose writers of both sexes, were born in the latter part of the reign of Henry IV., or during that of Louis XIII. Side by side with the great vices of those reigns, the talent and genius that were so fully developed under the regency of Anne of Austria and the first years of the reign of Louis XIV., gradually budded and expanded. Even those literary celebrities of the latter years of the century, who were most free from that spirit of adulation which grew out of Louis' belief in himself as a demi-god, at least, and which fettered the genius of such men as Racine, and made the muse of Molière the apologist of the vices of the monarch, were formed under the

Henry IV.

auspices, or after the example, of their predecessors who had flourished under the regency. To achieve success under the "Grand Monarque," it was far less necessary to merit it than to secure his favour, and this could only be done by chanting pæans of praise in his honour, and offering the incense of flattery at his shrine, amidst the gross fumes of which genius was too often stifled.

Beyond learned treatises on dry, dreary subjects, and no less dreary and voluminous theological writings, there was little or no literature in the time of Henry IV., but licentious poems and satires. But such writers who did take this lighter pen in hand, employed it, both in that and the succeeding reign, far more frequently to satirize and lecture the king than to flatter him. And Henry, especially, took this freedom of speech in good part. If, incorrigible sinner as he was, his morals were not improved by it, he, at all events, was amused. For he is said often to have read these productions, and greatly to have enjoyed such fun as there was in them, but never attempted to restrain the excessive license of the writers. Such toleration must have had a beneficial influence on the authors of that higher caste of literature which succeeded the "journals and satires" of Henry's day. The dramatist or poet could more freely give the rein to imagination, and infuse more real spirit and *verve* into his subject when untrammeled by the necessity of portraying, disguised under the name of some hero of antiquity, the hypothetical virtues and perfections of a pompous and vainglorious royal patron.

When Marie de Médicis was invested with absolute powers, and began her stormy career as queen-regent, she distributed pensions and places and titles with a very lavish hand, in order to gain over to her interests those friends of Henry who were opposed to her assumption of the regency. But in immediately bestowing a pension of five hundred *écus* upon Malherbe, she was prompted by a higher appreciation of the merits of the poet than Henry was capable of. She was ambitious, not only of governing France, but of governing grandly; and her ideas were grand though she had no grandeur in her character, and possessed none of the qualities for judiciously governing. She desired popularity, but was deficient in the tact necessary to acquire it, and had no winning graciousness or charm in her manners; but in her love of the Muses and *les beaux arts*, she was a true daughter of the Médici.

Malherbe has been called "the father of modern French poetry." His odes and sonnets are often licentious in tone, as were the manners of the age, but there is a grace and charm in much of his verse due to the perfection and purity with which he wrote the French language. Boileau considered Malherbe the first French author whose writings afforded an example of "the power of words rightly placed." Though a Court poet, Malherbe was poor. Henry very parsimoniously repaid the laureate's graceful and frequently charming stanzas, idealizing the attractions of the *belles*, both *brunes* and *blondes*, by whom his royal master by turns was enslaved. When, sonnet in hand, the poor poet appeared before the king, he is said almost to have asked an alms for it.

Malherbe's known sensitiveness to any deviation from the purity of the language, when spoken as well as written, is shown by an anecdote told of him, whether it be strictly true or not. He had been prevailed on, when near his end, to be confessed by a priest. The good father afterwards proceeded to expatiate, in language neither classical nor poetical, on the joys awaiting the dying man in heaven. Malherbe listened, evidently much disturbed in mind. The priest attributed it to conscience awakened by his eloquence, and became more earnest, and, as he thought, more impressive. The old poet could endure it no longer. Raising himself in his bed, he exclaimed, " Improve your style, sir! You have disgusted me with the joys of heaven!" then fell back exhausted on his pillow. An old nurse sat by the bedside ; she had been much edified to hear of the joys of heaven. Now she rose, looked sadly at the priest, and whispered, " Poor man! poor man!

His head is quite gone, sir. Only an hour ago he raved at me, even worse, sir, even worse, and called out, 'Who is your authority for that word?' though I spoke to him quite kind and civil. Poor man, his head is gone!"

Another *protégé* of Marie de Médicis (no poet of that day was without his patron) was the poet and epigrammatist, Ogier de Gombauld. He was as solicitous as Malherbe himself that the purity of the French language should be strictly maintained, and, as a means of ensuring it, proposed to the French Academy, of which he was one of the first members, that the academicians should bind themselves by oath to use no words that a majority of the society had not approved. Marie de Médicis gave him a pension of twelve hundred *écus*. But Marie's pensioners were unfortunate; the amount they received fluctuating with her fluctuating fortunes, until payment ceased altogether, and their royal patroness was herself an indigent wanderer, dependent on the sympathy and charity of foreigners. De Gombauld was a younger son of a noble Protestant family, and no expectation of court favour, poor though he was, induced him to change the Reformed for the Roman faith. He was born in the persecuting days of Charles IX., and lived far into the reign of Louis XIV., attaining to nearly a hundred years. His works, and especially his epigrams, had considerable vogue and success in their day.

To De Gombauld, Malherbe, Vaugelas, and Jean Louis de Balzac, the French language owes much of its beauty, clearness, and harmony. The *société d'élite* of the Hôtel de Rambouillet, whose example afterwards gave a tone of refinement to French society generally, imparted the same polished elegance also to the language, and purged it of those *grossièretés* which Molière and others would have retained, qualifying their indecencies by such terms as *naïveté* and *franchise*. But even Molière was compelled to abandon, in his later productions, some few of the coarse expressions that hitherto had found so much favour with him. And it was in deference to an authority which, though he rebelled against it, proved greater than his own; the purer literary taste that *préciosité* — a word unknown to the French language until late in the century — notwithstanding some affectations, had been the means of diffusing far beyond the circles of Rambouillet and its successors.

In the early years of the seventeenth century the ladies improved their minds, or sought amusement in leisure hours, by reading the works of Rabelais, or the poems of Ronsard. They had besides, as a corrective, "Philothée," a religious novel, by St. Jean Damoscène. It was called "Le roman des dévots," *par excellence*. "Amours d'Euryale et de Lucrèce," written by Pope Pius II., and therefore, no doubt, very edifying, if not very amusing, also retained favour, and a place on the scantily furnished bookshelves of *les dames châtelaines.*

A few months before the death of Henry IV. the first volume of "Astrée" appeared, a romance by the Marquis d'Urfé. From the extraordinary influence it had on the manners of the day, it is considered to have initiated that change in them which was confirmed by the society that met at the Hôtel de Rambouillet some years later. "Astrée" is a pastoral allegory, and describes the *amours platoniques* of the author, interspersed with many episodes of the gallantries of the court of Henry IV. But it is perfectly pure in tone. The characters are numerous, and it would be difficult to select, where all are important, a hero and heroine; but the title suggests the latter, and the author was known to be the former. Shepherds and shepherdesses are the principal personages, who, in long and rather vague conversations, and dissertations of unconscionable length, set forth the delights of chaste love, and the joys of an *honnête amitié.* Their language is sentimental in the extreme, and thus suited to the subject of their discourse; but affectations abound, and the high-flown expressions and dogmatic tone of some of the speakers give one the idea that these shepherds and shepherdesses are really only courtiers and sophists in disguise. The adventures of this rambling company are, however, numerous, and often amusing.

To retain popularity, as "Astrée" did, for upwards of half a century, a work must necessarily possess some merit. Boileau speaks of it as "*une narration vive et fleurie, ses caractères finement marqués, agréablement variés et bien suivis.*" "Astrée" was published in five quarto volumes, which appeared in succession, at irregular intervals, in the course of fifteen years; ten elapsed between the publication of the first and second volumes. The first was dedicated to Henry IV., who was pleased with the work. He received it but a short time before his assassination, and as he was then confined to his bed by gout, he desired it to be read to amuse him. The new species of gallantry "Astrée" introduced to his notice met with his approval, for though differing so greatly from his own, it coincided with it in one respect — it inculcated a system that made woman the object of universal homage.

The personal history of the Marquis d'Urfé has some romance in it. Henry had a strong aversion to him. He was one of the Leaguers, and, refusing to submit, was made prisoner of war. Soon after he escaped. Being a remarkably handsome man, witty in conversation, *distingué* in manners, Marguérite, Henry's wife, had fallen deeply in love with him. But the marquis was at that time the despairing slave of a hopeless passion for the celebrated beauty Diane de Châteaunormand, who, by an arrangement between his and her family, had become the wife of his elder brother. D'Urfé was, therefore, insensible to the fascinations of Marguérite. The cause of his melancholy being made known to her, her interest in him increased, and as it was evident that his heart was irrevocably disposed of, she contrived that he should soon be on his way to the court of Turin, his family being related to the House of Savoy. The lovelorn marquis then determined to become a knight of Malta. No sooner had he taken his vow, than his brother, animated by religious zeal, was desirous of being freed from the marriage yoke, in order to enter the Church as a cloistered monk. His application to Rome was complied with, and the beautiful Diane was free. The younger D'Urfé now, in his turn, addressed himself to Rome, praying to be absolved from his vow of celibacy. Interest and money aiding him, his prayer was granted, and, by the same means, a dispensation obtained, enabling him to marry his brother's wife.

But disappointment awaited the unfortunate marquis. Diane had been willing to marry him, because it prevented the alienation of certain estates; but as to love, she had none to give to her rapturous and adoring swain. She was beautiful as early spring, but intensely selfish, her deepest feeling being great admiration of her own charms. Profoundly grieved at her insensibility to his devotion to her, D'Urfé left his *belle marquise* and retired to a distant estate, where he sought to soothe his wounded spirit by depicting the pure pleasures of an ideal love. The story of his romantic and unrequited passion, his deep melancholy, his secluded life, gave added interest and extraordinary vogue to his romance. The succeeding volumes were looked for with an anxiety that did not abate during the fifteen years that expectation was kept on the stretch, and they were all equally well received as the first. When D'Urfé had completed his fifth volume, he died. The story of his hapless love being told, his work in this world was finished. By his direction the last volume was published by his secretary. The learned Huet, Bishop of Avranches, who wrote a work on " L'Origine des Romans," says that St. François de Sales read "Astrée" with intense delight, and named it "*le bréviaire des courtisans.*"

Arcadia became the rage ; the ladies were desirous of reproducing those scenes of pastoral love and idleness. But the gardens attached to the houses of the nobility in Paris, though large, were yet too confined, and their trees and shrubs too much clipped into formal devices to bear any resemblance to D'Urfé's Arcadian bowers and groves, sacred to gentle shepherds and shepherdesses in silks and lace. Yet the attempt to realize the pastoral life was really made in the faubourg by Vauquelin des Iveteaux, who had been

Governor of Caen, and was afterwards preceptor to the Duc de Vendôme, and to the dauphin. He had led a dissipated life, but, having read "Astrée," he was so charmed with the pastoral one that he resolved to forsake his irregularities, and to seek, in the evening of his days (he was then between sixty and seventy), the pure joys and peace that Arcadia promised.

He retired to a house with large gardens, which belonged to him, in the Faubourg St. Germain. There, dressed in the correct shepherd costume, with his rustic pipe, and by his side a pretty shepherdess, in pink and blue silk, and a crook trimmed with ribands and lace, he wandered about his grounds. The shepherd carried a lute, and when he and his *gentile amie* reposed beneath a shady tree, or lounged near a pond that did duty for a crystal stream, he played on his pipe while the lady twanged the lute and sang a few snatches of song. The gentleman led two lambs by a silken cord. They were "the milk-white flock," and lay at the feet of the shepherd and shepherdess when they sat down on a grassy slope to expatiate on the delights and pure joys of pastoral life and sentimental friendship. M. des Iveteaux lived in this way for some years, when weather permitted; and, as he lived to the age of ninety, it may be presumed that he found pastoral life pleasant and easy, and that rusticating agreed with him. He went out of the world to the sound of the lute and shepherd's pipe, accompanying an idyl of his own composing, for he was a tolerable poet. He thought that sweet simple sounds soothed the spirit when winging its flight from earth to the bowers of bliss. The end of this shepherd was peace.

"Astrée" had many imitators, but none that met with a like success, for none was inspired by a romantic passion such as guided the pen of D'Urfé. "Les Amours du Grand Alcandre" owed its origin to the success of "Astrée." The Princess de Conti (Louise de Lorraine) was its author, Henry IV. its hero. The work was satirical; but how thoroughly gross-minded the age must have been when a woman of rank and influence, and with a great reputation for learning, selected as a theme for her pen the frightful depravity of Henry IV., with a view of rendering it diverting, under the guise of a pastoral romance, as light reading for her own sex. The princess herself had been the object of one of Henry's numerous but short-lived *grandes passions*. In the midst of this general corruption, one pure-minded woman, disgusted with the vice of the court, withdrew from it, and resolved to attempt the regeneration of society; that woman was the Marquise de Rambouillet.

CHAPTER V.

Betrothal of Catherine de Vivonne and the Count d'Angennes. — The Pisani Family. — The Nobles and Clergy. — Educated Women. — Marguérite de France. — Desire for Social Intercourse. — La Folie Rambouillet. — The Old Hôtel Pisani. — The Hôtel de Rambouillet. — The Salon Bleu. — The Luxembourg Palace. — The Marquise de Rambouillet. — Rising Influence of Rambouillet. — The Marquis de Racan. — Armand du Plessis. — The Ladies of the Rambouillet Circle.

IN the same year (the first of the seventeenth century) that Henry IV. married Marie de Médicis, Catherine de Vivonne, daughter of the Marquis Pisani, was betrothed to the Count d'Angennes, eldest son of the Marquis de Rambouillet. Catherine was then but twelve years of age. Four years after, their marriage was solemnized, and the young Countess d'Angennes was introduced to a court the most depraved in morals, the grossest and most unpolished in manners, of any in Europe. She was immediately appointed one of the *dames d'honneur* of the queen.

The Pisani family was of Italian origin, and distantly connected with that of the Médici, but had settled in France from the time of Francis I.

Several of its members had served in the French army; others had held offices of state. They had married into French families, had become thoroughly French in their sympathies, and for two generations past they were French by birth. The families of both Rambouillet and Pisani had belonged to that "*parti de milieu*" of moderate Catholics who had favoured the pretensions of Henry of Navarre to the throne. There were eight brothers D'Angennes, and none of them had joined the League. It was the eldest son of the eldest of these brothers who had married Catherine de Vivonne. He held a military command, and, naturally, was high in favour with the king.

The young countess inherited a very large fortune — an immense one, it was thought in those days. She had been brought up in much seclusion, and had become attached to sedentary pursuits. She was fond of reading and conversation, had some skill in painting and architectural drawing, acquired, probably, during a residence in Italy. The boisterous revels of the court afforded her no pleasure; those "*ballets de la reine, ballets du roi, ballets de lacour*," etc., in all of which, queen, king, courtiers and ladies, took each a character, and danced and sang — the royal band of six violins accompanying — to the best of their ability, no doubt, but, at all events, gleefully and lustily. For those grandees, of whom the greater number were in intellectual culture scarcely on a level with the rude and unlettered classes of the present day, found, like them, the keenest of their pleasures in noise and energetic movement. And there was plenty of this gross hilarity while Henry reigned.

The general clergy, in intelligence, morals, and manners, were about on a par with the laity. The canons of Notre Dame and the Sainte Chapelle were forever quarrelling and scuffling when they met, each claiming to take the *pas* of the other. Even several years later, when Louis XIII. solemnly placed France under the protection of the Virgin Mary, "in order that all his loyal subjects might be received into Paradise, such being his goodwill and pleasure," the Parliament and the members of the Chamber of Finance contended so vehemently for precedency in the procession, that they came to blows in the Cathedral of Notre Dame. When any unusual rise in the Seine occurred; any outbreak of plague or smallpox, from the general filthiness of the city; the fall of a bridge from the undue weight of its houses, or similar catastrophe; to prevent a recurrence of it, the jawbone of St. This, the finger-joint of St. That, and the body of poor old St. Denis, dragged from its coffin, were carried in procession to the shrine of some dilapidated image of the Virgin, who might be prevailed on, it was hoped, by prayers and presents to appease the

Divine wrath, to which the people were taught to ascribe their calamities.

Education, for the most part, was despised by the accomplished cavaliers and *grand seigneurs* of those days. Some few condescended to read and write; but in war, the duel, the chase, and the dance, all aspired to acquit themselves well.

Woman, not improbably, might be the cause of a war or a duel, but as she was not required to take part in it, and frequently did not join in the pleasures or hardships of the chase, she had generally more instruction and culture than the men of the period, and to this was chiefly owing the social pre-eminence she attained in France. The seclusion of the *vie de château* was as favourable to her acquirement of studious habits and the indulgence of literary tastes, as was the cloister to the intellectually gifted monk. Many women knew something of Latin, if only so much as enabled them to follow the sense of the prayers in their *livres d'heures*. This little often led to the further study of the language, and the attainment of considerable proficiency in it. Marguérite de France, Henry's first wife, is said to have replied to the Latin address of the Bishop of Cracow (one of the ambassadors deputed to offer the crown of Poland to her brother, the Duke of Anjou) with so much fluency and eloquence, that he was no less delighted than surprised by it.

The Countess d'Angennes appears to have had

less knowledge of Latin, as it is stated that her desire to read Virgil led her to study the language, but that ill-health compelled her to discontinue it. She, however, was well acquainted with Italian and Spanish. The latter was acquired in Spain, whither she accompanied her husband. She brought thence to Paris that fashion of alcoves which she introduced into her own hôtel, and which so long remained, and to a certain degree still continues, a favourite arrangement in French bedrooms. After the birth of her daughter (in later years the celebrated Julie d'Angennes), she withdrew from the Louvre, and returned to it no more, except on the occasion when she was named by Henry one of the *dames d'honneur* to attend Marie de Médicis at her coronation.

The Marquise de Rambouillet (her husband's father had lately died) was then in her twentieth year — "*belle, bonne et spirituelle.*" Other ladies to whom culture had imparted a refinement of manners out of harmony with the discord and scandal that reigned at court, also held aloof from its coarse pleasures and noisy gaieties; for at that time a strong and general desire was awakened amongst persons of rank and easy fortune for social communication, intimate and varied, yet more polished than hitherto had existed in France. The social instinct was born, but as yet its influence was small; for there was no society apart from the court; no *salons* thrown open for the reception of distinguished *littérateurs*, and no social *réunions*. The theatre — the favourite amusement of the marquise — was open only now and then; the performances also were occasional, and *loges à l'année* not then introduced. The French Academy was not yet founded, and the men who were to shed most lustre upon it were either unborn, still unknown to fame, or mere youths, and their talents immature.

But the Hôtel de Rambouillet was about to be erected — that renowned hôtel, destined to welcome and foster rising genius and talent; to assemble rank, beauty, wit, worth and learning in its celebrated *salon bleu*, and by the influence of its *société d'élite* on the manners and literature of the age to achieve a social revolution, and to acquire lasting fame in the republic of letters. Meanwhile "*Je me figure*," writes Roederer, "*que jamais on n'eut autant besoin de se parler de s'épancher, en France ni ailleurs qu'à cette époque.*"

French writers differ greatly in their accounts of the famous Hôtel de Rambouillet, as regards its situation and date of erection. Not a vestige of it now remains to fix either with certainty. It has sometimes been confounded with the Hôtel Rambouillet built by the rich financier, father of Rambouillet de la Sablière, the poet, and husband of Madame de la Sablière, celebrated in the verse of La Fontaine and the Marquis de la Fare. This edifice was generally known at that time as

"La Folie Rambouillet." It was built on his estate at the village of Reuilly, where now the Rue de Rambouillet joins the Avenue Monmesnil. Its gardens were celebrated for their extent and beauty. Others make the old Hôtel Pisani, re-christened and embellished, do duty for the hôtel that was built from the designs of the marquise herself. Tallemant des Réaux, who was an intimate friend of the marquise, and a frequenter of her *salon*, and therefore should be correctly informed, says: "Her father sold the old Hôtel Pisani, in 1606, for 345,000 liv., and the Cardinal de Richelieu, in 1624, bought it for 30,000 *écus*, when it was taken down, and the Palais Cardinal, afterward Palais Royal, built on its site." It was an ancient domain; in appearance, almost a feudal *château*.

The new Hôtel de Rambouillet was built in grounds or gardens already belonging to the family in the Rue St. Thomas du Louvre. The marquise herself was its architect. No design that was offered pleased her, and her own was entirely followed; yet there were then in Paris several Italian architects of repute, invited by Marie de Médicis, who, on assuming the regency, determined on building herself a palace, in imitation of her relative and predecessor, Catherine.

The Hôtel de Rambouillet was of red brick and slate, with embrasures, cornices, friezes, architraves, and pilasters of freestone. These materials were then generally employed for large buildings, and were thought to combine well and to harmonize agreeably to the eye.* Rambouillet was of less extent than many of the hôtels of the nobility; but the space at command was so skilfully turned to account, the apartments so admirably proportioned and disposed with so much art, that the effect was that of a mansion more spacious than many that were in fact larger, but were less judiciously and conveniently arranged.

There were four principal *salons* leading into each other on the ground-floor; an arrangement which, with their high, wide doors and long windows, reaching from floor to ceiling, was first introduced by the marquise, and afterwards copied in the Petit Luxembourg, in Richelieu's palace, and the yet unfinished houses of the Place Royale. Indeed, Rambouillet served as a model for many of the châteaux and palaces of France in the seventeenth century. The loftiness of its *salons*, its circular staircase, leading to the *corps de logis*, or range of rooms on the first floor, with the long line of doors at equal distances, and facing each other, were all novelties that met with general approval and adoption. The gardens extended the whole length of the suite of *salons*, affording

---

* When the rich bourgeois built themselves houses after the same fashion, this combination of red, white, and slate colour immediately went out of favour, as giving the appearance of a house built of cards.

a pleasant view, as well as light and air. The *salons* were thrown open or closed, according as the society was more or less numerous; but all were superbly furnished.

The marquise is said to have been the first to innovate on the custom of colouring or painting the rooms of a red tint or a tawny dark yellow. Hence the admiration bestowed on the "*salon bleu*," apart from its being the principal *salle de réunion*. Its walls were hung with blue velvet, panelled in borders of gold. The furniture was of the same material, relieved by gold fringes and lace. "The air was perfumed with the odour of flowers, arranged in beautiful vases and baskets, and in such profusion that eternal spring seemed to reign there." In the evening the *salons* were lighted with lamps of Venetian glass, also first seen at Rambouillet; and there were splendid Italian cabinets, filled with the choicest and rarest specimens of delicate sculpture, scarce enamels, gems, and other articles of *virtu*. Amongst the many treasures of the *salon bleu* was a spinet, a marvel of its kind, brought by the marquise from Italy. It was exquisitely painted with flowers and birds, and inlaid with turquoise, gold, and pearl.* It is probable that

* The South Kensington Museum has a spinet of the latter part of the sixteenth century. It is of Italian workmanship, and may resemble the Rambouillet spinet, though perhaps less richly ornamented; yet it is an interesting work of art. It belonged to an Italian princess of that period.

its ornamentation enchanted the eye more than its music the ear. The lute and the théorbe were the instruments then in vogue for the voice; the violins for a dance; but whether Rambouillet danced we have not been told. Only the stately minuet could have found favour there; certainly no "*ballet du roi*" of the court of that time. The opera was not yet introduced into France, and Lulli was not yet born.

"Rambouillet was built in the time of le Maréchal d'Ancre." It was completed about 1614, when the park and gardens of the Luxembourg Palace were being laid out and planted. The palace itself was not begun until the following year; for although Marie de Médicis had employed the architect De Brosse to furnish the designs, they were only finally accepted after having been submitted to almost every architect of note in France and Italy, and some few of the alterations they suggested adopted. They were also inspected, at the queen's request, by Madame de Rambouillet, and every part of her hôtel was visited by De Brosse before the works at the Luxembourg were begun. But the architect's visit was intended probably as a compliment only to the talented marquise; for De Brosse proposed to recall the style of the Pitti Palace — where the queen had usually resided while at the court of her father, the Grand Duke of Tuscany — in the *façades* of the sumptuous Palais de Luxembourg. And its interior arrangement naturally would differ greatly from that of the private mansion of one of the nobility.

Madame de Rambouillet was about twenty-six years of age when her hôtel was furnished and ready for occupation. We learn from writers of the day that she was very tall and of dignified carriage. (All the family, both sons and daughters, were so much above the middle height, that they were called familiarly, "*les sapins de Rambouillet.*") Her features were regular, her eyes and complexion fine. Whenever she is mentioned in contemporary epistolary writings and memoirs, it is always with respect and admiration — an agreement in opinion of which they afford scarcely another instance, when referring to any celebrated person of the time. Mademoiselle de Scudéry speaks of her as "beautiful, witty, gentle, and generous; constant in friendship, good, just, and pure." No foreigner of any distinction visited Paris but sought an opportunity of paying her the homage so justly due to her; and so highly was her judgment esteemed on subjects connected with literature and art, that not only would poets submit their verses to her, but often skilled workmen sought her approval of their choicest artistic productions.

Rambouillet only gradually acquired its great

influence and eminence; it did not immediately become the tribunal of language and taste, the centre "*d'une société polie.*" It was checked at the outset by the spirit of discord that reigned in the capital. Marie de Médicis had not only proved incapable of governing the kingdom, but had allowed herself to be governed by arrogant and unprincipled Italian favourites, who filled every lucrative office of state, and were intent on enriching themselves at the expense of the oppressed people. Many noble families had withdrawn from the court in disgust, and retired to their *châteaux* in the provinces. But the poets Malherbe and Ogier de Gombauld, with Vaugelas, the classical writer, and Jean Louis de Balzac — then not more than twenty years of age — were among the first of the *gens de lettres* of that day who frequented the Hôtel de Rambouillet. The young Marquis de Racan was also of their number; he afterwards wrote the life of Malherbe, having been a disciple of the old poet, who instructed him in the art of versification. From reading D'Urfé's "Astrée," Racan had become imbued with the same sentimental and romantic ideas. He either was, or fancied himself, passionately in love with the marquise, and poured forth the story of his woes in his "Bergeries," the most popular of his poetical works. He also depicted his passion and the coldness and indifference of his *bergère*, Arthenice

(Malherbe's anagram of Catherine), in a pastoral play. Boileau, in his "Art Poétique," says:

> "Malherbe d'un héro peut vanter les exploits;
> Racan chanter Phillis, les bergers et les bois."

Racan cured himself of his hopeless passion for the *belle marquise* by going for a time to the wars and afterwards taking a wife.

By adopting the name of Arthenice, Madame de Rambouillet has been considered to have given the first example of an affectation which was afterwards largely imitated. All women of any celebrity had their "*noms de Parnasse*," so called by La Fontaine, who christened so many of the Sylvias, Phillises, etc., of the day, the Hôtel de Rambouillet itself being known as "Le Parnasse Français."

Armand du Plessis, Bishop of Luçon, afterwards Cardinal de Richelieu, but then almoner to the queen, was one of the early *habitués* of the Hôtel, and more than once took part there in the discussion of a thesis, whose subject was love. Du Plessis went to Rome in 1609, to be created a bishop, when he was under the prescribed age by two years. Pope Paul V. having inquired what was his age, Du Plessis did not hesitate to make a false statement to his Holiness. But when the ceremony was ended, he confessed that he had told an untruth, and prayed that the pope would grant him absolution, which he did, remarking, "Questo giovane sere un gran furbo."

The names of the ladies who first formed part of the learned society of Rambouillet are not mentioned in the writings of the time. We learn only that Madame la Princesse de Condé was one of them, and generally they may then have been more distinguished for their rank than learning. Ségrais, at a later date, when the Hôtel was at the height of its reputation, says, "Although the rank of Madame de Rambouillet was below that of duchess, she was held in such high esteem that princesses waived all considerations of etiquette for the pleasure of assisting at her *réunions*."

CHAPTER VI.

Louis XIII. — The Brothers D'Albert. — Revels à l'Italienne. — Le Maréchal d'Ancre. — La Perle du Marais. — The Hôtel Lesdiguières. — The Cours de la Reine. — Statue of Henry IV. — Prevalence of Duelling. — The Queen a Peacemaker. — The Double Spanish Marriage. — Quadrilles d'Arioste. — Marriage Fêtes. — The Girl-queen, Anne of Austria. — Marguérite de France.

LOUIS XIII. makes but a sorry figure on the page of history. The stormy, imperious, and imprudent Queen-regent, Marie de Médicis, and the powerful, energetic, and implacable Minister, De Richelieu, overshadow his reign, and are throughout it far more important personages than the gloomy, weak, and irresolute king. Louis was surnamed "The Just," but not for the justice of his acts. The surname was given to him by the astrologers who were in attendance at his birth to cast his nativity — as was the common custom in that superstitious age — and who announced that the royal infant had come into the world under the zodiacal sign of the Balance. As a child, he was obstinate, disobedient, and sullen, qualities which Marie endeavoured to have flogged out of him. She spared not the rod, and at times, with her own plump white hand, administered the needful correction.

His youthful Majesty was rarely willing to say his prayers, in spite of the whipping he knew was in store for him; yet often, when to work on his fears the terrible punishment awaiting such miserable sinners in another world was too forcibly set before him, he would suddenly, in terror, sink on his knees, and hurriedly and incoherently repeat his orisons. His frame of mind at the time was no doubt similar to that attributed to him in after years when it was said, in allusion to the urgency of his devotions, that "no man loved God less or feared the prince of darkness more." His education was greatly neglected. After the old French fashion, he was surrounded with young pages of noble family; obsequious playmates, who had been taught to yield to all his humours and childish caprices. Louis was a stammerer, and much of his ill-temper, reserve, and gloom may be attributed to that defect. His favourites were the two brothers D'Albert (originally Alberti, of Florence). They were many years older than Louis, but had gained his favour by their skill in falconry. Louis, like his father, loved the sound of the hunting-horn, the movement of the chase, the forests of Fontainebleau, and after the manner of a page of the middle ages, devoted himself to the training of hawks. He had learned of Charles d'Albert to make nets, thongs, overalls of leather, and various articles required for hawking and hunting. As Louis grew up he displayed, says the caustic Tallemant des Réaux, "*Cent vertus de valet, et pas une vertu de maître.*"

The queen-regent meanwhile was giving a ceaseless round of public *fêtes*, revels *à l'Italienne*, carrousels, and tournaments, in which the laws and rules of the old *chevalerie* were revived, and with extraordinary splendour of knightly accoutrements, embroidered banners, etc. There were fireworks also, and at Vincennes combats of animals. Vincennes had a menagerie then, and an open court with tiers of seats for spectators of the fight. Marie de Médicis was courting popularity both for herself and the Concini. The council of regency was divided into the Italian party and the party of the French nobility. She wished to gain over the latter, and to ingratiate herself with the populace. The Maréchal d'Ancre (Concini) had introduced *les jeux de bague* and other games requiring skill and dexterity. In these he acquitted himself with remarkable grace and elegance. He was a handsome man, and far more polished in manners than Henry's rude warrior friends. These rough soldiers regarded both him and his sports, and all the tribe of les Gondi, Concini, Alberti, and Strozzi, predecessors of les Mazarini, with ineffable contempt. But the ladies looked on with favour, smiled on the Italian, bestowed plaudits upon him, and playfully pelted him with flowers, perfumed gloves, and handkerchiefs steeped in essences.

Most of these *fêtes* took place in the Place Royale, which was entirely finished in 1616. Henry had intended it for a splendid bazaar, in imitation of the Place St. Marc at Venice, and the houses for bathing establishments after the oriental fashion. But the *beau monde* took a fancy to the Place Royale. This immense quadrilateral, with its four wide roads for horses and carriages, and causeways for foot passengers, was at that time one of the greatest improvements of Paris, and from the elegant style of its architecture, its greatest embellishment. The interior and exterior of the spacious houses were finished and decorated to harmonize with their new destination, and the *haute noblesse* took up their quarters there. When the weather was fine, the gardens were thronged with cavaliers and ladies, who sauntered through the carefully clipped elmtree walks bordered with box cut into hearts, true lovers' knots and various other devices. Two stone fountains sculptured with tritons, dolphins, etc., stood in the gardens,—one at each end. The galleries of the surrounding houses afforded a covered walk, opening on the square by a hundred and forty-four arches. La Place Royale was considered "La perle du marais," and that new faubourg (Paris was not then divided into its twenty *quartiers*) became renowned later on in the seventeenth century. Rank and fashion, wealth and beauty, dwelt there, and *une société spirituelle* assembled in the noble *salons* of its spacious mansions. Delicate carvings, exquisite paintings enriched the cornices, doors, and ceilings; Venetian mirrors, Florentine tapestry adorned the walls; silks, damasks, and rich brocatelle covered the gilded *fauteuils* and *canapés*.

In the Rue St. Antoine and neighbouring streets were also several splendid private mansions or hôtels of the nobility. Some two or three were of the previous century, and decorated by the celebrated sculptor, Jean Goujon. The Hôtel Béthune, the residence of the Minister Sully, was built for him at the beginning of Henry IV.'s reign by Ducerceau, on a part of the site of the Palais des Tournelles. Its façade is finely sculptured. But of all the hôtels of the Rue St. Antoine, the Hôtel Lesdiguières was the most celebrated for the splendour of its furniture. Sauval speaks of the principal *salle* as "*plus que royale*." Its hangings were of brocade woven with gold thread, with mother-of-pearl and coral worked in, in arabesques. The greater part of the furniture was of massive silver, beautifully chased, and the parts in relief gilded. There were Venetian cabinets of the most exquisite workmanship and elegant design. Vases and girandoles of rock crystal, ancient bronzes, rare marbles and ivories, rich tapestry, and valuable paintings. This celebrated hôtel gave its name to a street, but no vestige of the building now exists. Its treasures were dispersed, and the family is extinct. But the Hôtel Béthune, or Sully, remains an interesting specimen of French architecture, of the latter part of the sixteenth and early seventeenth century.

The promenade known as "the Cours de la Reine" was, by order of Marie de Médicis, planted with four rows of trees, and thrown open to the public. It was of the length of a Roman stadium; about the eighth of an English mile. The Maréchal de Bassompierre asked and obtained permission to pave the slopes with freestone at his own expense. He also placed at each end of the drive a handsome iron gate supported by sculptured stone-work. The Cours de la Reine was the resort of the court and the *beau monde* during the warm summer evenings.

The queen-regent was very desirous of embellishing Paris. In the first year of her regency the little king laid the first stone of the buildings designed for the College of France, which had existed in name from the time of Francis I., but "local habitation" it had none, until Marie, sixty years after, gave it one. The aqueduct of Arcueil, the first construction of the kind in

France, was also due to her, and the grand pavilion over the entrance to the Louvre. The equestrian statue of Henry IV. on the Pont Neuf was a present to the queen from the Grand Duke of Tuscany. Cosmo II. put it on board a vessel that went ashore on a mud-bank, just after leaving the harbour. With much labour it was transferred uninjured to another, which carried it safely to Havre. It arrived in 1614, but was not placed on the bridge until some years after. Louis laid the first stone of the marble pedestal. The four figures representing the four quarters of the world were sculptured by Pierre de Franqueville. This statue of Henry IV. was the first statue erected in Paris to the honour of any French king. It was the work of the famous Giovanni da Bologna.

In 1615 the queen laid the first stone of her Palace of Luxembourg, which she was destined never to inhabit. The Rue de Seine, leading to it, was also begun. It was outside the old limits, beyond which Paris was gradually extending itself, especially on the north side of the river. The new bridge, Pont Marie, and the houses of the Ile St. Louis — built by M. Marie, a rich bourgeois of Paris, who obtained a grant of the site from the queen — as well as many other changes and improvements in the city and faubourgs, were all either made by order of Marie de Médicis or were approved by her.

Duelling then prevailed to so great an extent — notwithstanding that by a recent law it was prohibited, and heavy penalties enacted against transgressors — that it was necessary for every *gentilhomme* to be a skilful swordsman. So sensitive were the honourable gentlemen of that age, that it was not unusual for them to have to call on each other in the course of a conversation "to eat their words," or draw their swords, more than once or twice in the day. Some *preux chevalier* took offence at the indiscreet utterance of another *preux*, and only shedding of blood could atone for outraged honour. Apology was of course out of the question. The consequence was that the fencing schools — they were called academies then — were very numerously attended. An old writer boasts of there being six academies in the Faubourg St. Germain alone, and doubts whether any other city in Europe possessed so many. These academies were presided over by old officers of small means, but who, if skilful with the sword, made a very good income by their teaching.

"The manner of carrying the rapier * was with the point upwards, the hand on the guard at the side of the hip, so as slightly to raise the cloak, as if to present a continual menace of crossing swords in a duel, and of a meeting at two paces'

---

* Collet's ' Cavaliers du Règne de Louis XIII."

distance in the Pré de la Bastille." Duels often took place in the streets; the cause, questions of etiquette, or perhaps family hatreds and feuds, for a spirit of great disorder reigned throughout society — Catholic against Protestant, family against family. When collisions of this kind occurred, the queen often personally interfered, either to reconcile the combatants or to order them to disarm and remain in their hôtels until anger had cooled down and they had come to their senses. When she succeeded in pacifying the aggrieved parties, or in adjusting the difficulty that was the cause of the combat, she took great credit to herself, and expressed her satisfaction in council. But her peace was often troubled, and considerable annoyance caused her by scurrilous pamphlets, and pasquinades after the Italian fashion. The manners of her court were satirized, her government of the kingdom censured.

However, her domestic government continued strong, pressing less heavily on her second son, Gaston, than on Louis, who was now fourteen. He was of age, and might, had he so chosen, have taken the government of the kingdom into his own hands. A bride, a few days younger than himself, was on her way to France. The double Spanish marriage was arranged, and his sister, the Princess Elizabeth, a child of twelve, was also on her journey to Spain, to marry the Prince of the Asturias, afterwards Philip IV.

From the extreme punctiliousness of both the French and the Spaniards on this occasion — the French *grand seigneur* and the Spanish grandee, deputed to exchange the brides, each fearing to compromise the dignity of his nation if he advanced nearer than the other to the frontiers — it seemed likely that the poor children would have to return to their respective nurseries instead of continuing their journey and being married. But at last the exchange was effected, and Anne of Austria was conducted to Paris by her youthful bridegroom. She was a fine tall girl, a Spanish *blonde*, wanting yet two or three summers for the full development of her beauty.

The royal marriages gave occasion for a renewal of those *fêtes* and entertainments in which the queen-regent took as much delight as did her partizans at court or the Parisian people. "Quadrilles d'Arioste" were performed in the Place de Carrousel; Roland, Rénaud de Montauban, and the rest of the characters being represented by *les grands seigneurs*. The *galanterie Castellane* had also its representatives, in compliment to the young queen. Groups, too, of mythological personages came rushing on the scene in enormous triumphal cars drawn by monstrous beasts — something in the style of a Mardi-gras procession. Their mission was to proclaim to the revellers the astounding feats of *le puissant roi* Louis XIII. — yet to be accomplished, of course, but which were clearly seen to be looming in the distance.

Mars announced him as the conquering hero of the future; Jupiter, as the mightiest of the mighty rulers of France, and Minerva stepped in to declare that wisdom should guide him when he let loose his thunderbolts. "Glorious Apollo" appeared to tell of his love for, and his enlightened patronage of the arts; and the chaste huntress, goddess Diana, to vaunt his prowess in the chase. But when beautiful Venus with her wicked little son drove in, in her sumptuous car — doves and loves without number fluttering around her — she had a victory already achieved to congratulate the youthful but potent monarch upon. Gracefully she waved her hand, and kissed the rosy tips of her fingers as she bent towards *la belle Espagnole*, who, all radiant with delight, sat *en reine* by the side of her gloomy young spouse. She, poor girl, enjoyed the gay and festive scene: the boy-husband was thoroughly bored by it.

But the true hero of it all seemed to be he who had had the largest share in devising these revels, and took a conspicuous part in them,— the graceful, smiling Concini. Charles d'Albert — to whom the maréchal had just given the governorship of Amboise — drew the young king's attention to this, and roused his jealousy of the usurper, as he called him, of his power. "Ballets féeriques" were danced at the Louvre by the youthful nobility, who were dressed as fairies, cupids, and angels. Theatrical representations occupied their elders. Marie was exceedingly fond of plays, and the noise, the movement, the dress and display, the profusion and the lavish expense the celebration of these miserable marriages occasioned were a source of delight and gratification to her.

Masses of the people assembled, and thronged the streets and the open spaces near the palace, to catch a glimpse of the plumes and slashed doublets, the ruffs and the ruffles, the lace-trimmed funnel boots and gold-embroidered *chausses* of the *grands seigneurs*, as well as to admire the pretty painted faces, the frizzy *coiffures*, the feathers and diamonds, the velvets and satins, and fine Venetian point-lace of the *belles dames* of the *haute noblesse*. But far prettier, more interesting, and most novel sight of all, was the girl-queen, in her Spanish mantilla, archly smiling, and coquettishly flirting her Moorish fan. She was taken through Paris in a new and finely-painted royal carriage — the queen-mother and the young king accompanying her, and as many courtiers and ladies as the capacious vehicle would accommodate. These revels were the last that Marguérite de France took any part in. She died in the course of the year, aged sixty-three. After her return to France, by Henry's permission, she built a large mansion in the Pré aux Clercs, which had been for ages reserved for the recreation of the students of the various colleges. They rebelled at her appropriation of it, and a serious disturbance was the result. Marguérite lived there in reckless extravagance, causing much scandal. She lighted up her hôtel every night with hundreds of candles, making it quite a brilliant object in dark, dirty Paris, where robberies and assassinations were nightly committed with impunity; for the streets had no other lighting than the occasional glimmer of a candle that some householder put in his window, with good intent, to enlighten the footsteps of his neighbours, but whose only effect was to make the darkness more visible. Marguérite de France kept open house at this time, and looked for admiration as in the days of her youth. She was thickly rouged up to the eyes, wore a flowing wig of black hair, and generally an old-fashioned *houppelande* or long gold-braided *casaque*. She and Marie de Médicis were on excellent terms, and Marie every year paid Marguérite's debts.

CHAPTER VII.

Revolt of M. le Prince. — Elenora Galagai. — Concini's great Wealth. — "The Accursed Jews." — Assassination of Concini. — His Wife Burnt as a Sorceress. — The Queen-regent Exiled. — Armand du Plessis. — Marie's Return. — The Luxembourg. — Rubens' Twenty-four Paintings. — "The Day of Dupes." — Escape of Marie of Brussels. — Richelieu rules France. — Marie in Poverty and Exile.

THE unusual stir and commotion which the royal marriages had occasioned in Paris were taken advantage of by M. le Prince (Henri de Condé) to assemble those of his partizans among the French nobles who were most strongly opposed to the Maréchal d'Ancre, and had determined on his overthrow. But their plot was either ill-timed or ill-conducted, for instead of deposing the Italian, the prince himself was arrested in the Louvre and sent to Vincennes. Others of the party were lodged in the Bastille, or were banished to their châteaux, and Marie and her minister congratulated themselves on this triumph, as they believed it to be, over their foes.

The Prince and Princess de Condé lived by no means on amicable terms. She had resented his forcible removal of her to Brussels to elude the pursuit of Henry IV., whose mad passion had rather flattered her vanity than displeased her. She had then used every means in her power to obtain a divorce, but the prince opposed it, though the marriage had been urged upon him, only that Henry might take his wife from him.

After the king's assassination the prince brought her back to Paris, but their estrangement still continued. A change, however, seems to have come over the feelings of the princess when she heard of her husband's imprisonment, as she requested to be allowed to share his confinement. Her request was granted, and their reconciliation took place at Vincennes.

The wife of the Maréchal d'Ancre was Elenora Galagai. She was the foster-sister of Marie de Médicis, and accompanied her to France on her marriage with Henry. If writers of the time may be relied upon, Elenora was a most repulsively ugly woman; but it is more likely that her repulsiveness was in her character, and that she was intriguing, artful and haughty, though possessed of powers of mind that gave her great influence over the queen. Marie had a great affection for her, and married her to her secretary, Concini, the more effectually to promote the interests of both favourites. Warned by the increasing dissatisfaction of the nobles, and the loud complaints of the suffering people, of the constant imposition of new and burdensome taxes Elenora and her husband were secretly taking steps for transferring their immense wealth to Italy.

Concini possessed several fine châteaux in the provinces, and two or more in Paris, as well as marquisates with large estates, extensive and productive farms, and flourishing vineyards. All this property he proposed stealthily to turn into specie, and through the agency of some Italian Jews, who were invited by him to settle for a time in Paris, he looked forward to speedily doing so. "During the seven years of the government of the queen-regent," says a French writer, "Concini had amassed not less than fifteen hundred thousand escudi de Rome, from the sale of public offices and from oppressive taxation."

But the Jews! The pious were filled with horror, and crossed themselves devoutly at the mention of the word Jew, and the enlightened populace, generally, trembled lest the wrath of Heaven should be wreaked upon them when they learned that the "accursed Jews" were actually among them. An ancient law had banished them from France. The Italian Concini, the oppressor of the people, had brought them back; that vile race that had denied Jesus Christ! Outcasts from their country; wanderers on the face of the earth, condemned for their crime to be a "byword among the nations," and every man's hand to be against them, "a race leagued with the devil and the powers of darkness, who, in exchange for their souls, had taught them the secret of making gold." Some terrible calamity was looked for. The reliques, the virgins, the saints, all were appealed to, to exorcise the land and deliver France from the malignant influence and presence of the Jews.

It was at this juncture that the favourite of the king saw the desired opportunity of overthrowing the favourite of the queen-regent. It was difficult to make Louis take a resolution, but when taken, as difficult to move him either to change or to modify it. He would never enter into discussion; but the impediment in his speech may in a great degree account for that. By persistence, however, the favourite Charles' d'Albert prevailed on the king, in 1617, to sign a warrant for the arrest of the Maréchal d'Ancre. His scruples had arisen from filial respect — that feeling so strong in French families of all classes, even where, as in Louis' case, no great affection appears to exist. It was not easy to efface it, or to overcome his boyish fears of exciting the anger of his violent mother by an act of authority that deposed her favourite and took from her the government of the kingdom. But the warrant was signed, and Charles d'Albert was to succeed the maréchal as minister. When arrested Concini resisted, and drew his sword to defend himself. This had been foreseen and provided for. Five or six daggers were immediately unsheathed, and soon his body, bleeding and mangled, was thrown out to the populace, given up to the barbarities of a mob, more cruel, more revoltingly savage than beasts of prey.

Concini's wife, La Maréchale d'Ancre as she was called, was put on her trial as a sorceress, and for having, with the aid of necromancers and demons, cast a spell over the mind of the queen, and enriched herself and her husband by taking advantage of the infatuated imagination of her royal mistress. La Maréchale seems to have behaved with some dignity when arraigned before the enlightened tribunal commissioned to condemn her and to confiscate the property.

"Is it not true," said the learned judge "is it not true, wicked woman, that your influence over the queen-mother was gained by your spells and incantations?"

"It was gained," she replied, "by that power which strong minds naturally possess over the weak."

She was, however, condemned. She had been seen to ascend Catherine de Médicis's tower in the Hôtel de Soissons. This was accepted as proof positive of her guilt, and, accordingly, as a sorceress she was beheaded and burnt on the Place de Grève; that famous Place, which for centuries was by turns the scene of the public rejoicings and public executions of Paris — a crowd as great assembling to witness the horrors and sufferings of the latter as to gaze on the illuminations and fireworks, and to join in the dances of the former. The Hôtel de Ville figured no less prominently for upwards of three hundred years in the various commotions and outbreaks of popular fury in Paris; but it was left to the fanatics of the dark days of the commune to destroy that fine edifice and ornament of their city.

The death of the Concini closed the reign of Marie de Médicis. "I have reigned," she said, "for seven years over France; I now look only for a heavenly crown."

On the 4th of May, 1617, she left Paris for the Château de Blois, the place of exile assigned her. She wept bitterly when she found that Barbini, her Intendant du palais, was not allowed to accompany her, as she had requested. Louis, on the contrary, had never looked so radiant, so happy, so full of good-humour as on the day of her departure. He was then sixteen.

"*Enfin,*" he exclaimed, "*me voici roi!*"

Yet it was merely a *révolution du palais* that had taken place. Charles d'Albert was created Duc de Luynes; the confiscated property of the unfortunate maréchal became his successor's; the valuable jewels of his wife passed into the hands of the young Duchess de Luynes — the beautiful Mademoiselle Rohan Montbazon, afterwards the celebrated Duchesse de Chevreuse, and who was the first object of Louis' *amours platoniques*. The Concini being dethroned, the Alberti reigned in their stead, and poor Louis XIII. was no more king than before.

Armand du Plessis, Bishop of Luçon, had held the office of secretary under Maréchal d'Ancre, but on the assassination of his patron and the change in the government occurring he retired to Avignon and occupied himself in study and writing. Two years afterwards he was recalled, at the instance of De Luynes, who then ruled France and the king with a very high hand, and on whom all sorts of honours had been heaped, even to that of the distinguished post of Constable of France. Most of the ancient nobility had seceded from the court while the Concini were in the ascendant. De Luynes, to strengthen his position, invited them to return; he also liberated M. le Prince from Vincennes, in 1619. Two months before, the princess had given birth there to a daughter, Anne Geneviève de Bourbon, afterwards the celebrated Duchesse de Longueville, and sister of the Grand Condé, who was born in 1621.

Marie de Médicis had escaped from Blois to Angoulême; but as De Luynes was more disposed to show his power by being grandly gracious towards his enemies, and by conciliatory rather than by crushing measures, he contrived to make overtures of peace that proved acceptable to the queen-mother. The Bishop of Luçon effected a reconciliation between her and the king, and Marie returned to Paris after the signing of the treaty of Brissac.

The building of her palace of Luxembourg had progressed so rapidly during her absence that it was finished in 1620. It was then the most regular in its architecture of any of the royal residences. Its interior decorations, the cornices, architraves, etc., were the work of the first sculptors of the day, and much of its panelling, destroyed or removed during subsequent alterations, was adorned by the pencil of Poussin or Simon Vouet. The twenty-four large paintings — since transferred to the Louvre — of the chief events in the life of Marie de Médicis were, as is well known, executed by Rubens after the queen's return. Two only were painted in Paris and wholly by the great master himself, — that in which Minerva is counselling Henry IV. to take Marie de Médicis for a bride (advice the wisdom of which Henry would scarcely have endorsed), and the one representing the birth of Louis XIII. These two fine paintings have by some connoisseurs been considered the chefs-d'œuvre of the series. The others were sketched by Rubens in Paris, and painted at Antwerp, principally, if not entirely, by his pupils or assistants, with the exception of some finishing touches by the master's hand.

Peter Paul Rubens

Marie used to sit for hours together conversing with Rubens while he was engaged in painting. She had a great regard for him; and his learning and varied knowledge, as statesman, ambassador, and man of the world, as well as his great skill in his art, were fully appreciated by her.

It has been made a reproach to Marie de Médicis that a proposed second series of paintings, of which the career of Henry IV. was to furnish the subject, was not the first put in hand. Rubens is said to have prepared sketches for these pictures while in Paris, but that the subsequent misfortunes of his patroness prevented the carrying out of her project. It may, however, be doubted that it was ever entertained.

Most unexpectedly the Duc de Luynes died of camp fever while heading an expedition against the unfortunate Huguenots, and the queen-mother immediately resumed all her old ascendency over the weak mind of her son. She introduced her *surintendant*, the Bishop of Luçon, into the council, greatly against the wish of the king, who was shocked at the licentiousness of his life.

In 1622 the Bishop of Luçon became Cardinal de Richelieu. Marie, who had proposed to govern the kingdom through him, looked to find him pliant and subservient, as Concini had been. But Richelieu soon found means to possess himself of the whole authority of the crown, to use it, as his admirers say, for the benefit of the state and the glory of France.

The queen-mother, disappointed to find an opponent instead of an ally in the man whose advancement she had zealously promoted, with her usual violence complained of his conduct, and menaced him with the king's displeasure. Being compelled to desist from open antagonism, she joined in plots and intrigues to accomplish his overthrow. Their result to her was humiliation, to some of her accomplices death. After the famous "day of dupes," * 11th November, 1630, when it was for some hours believed, even by the queen-mother herself, that Richelieu's downfall was accomplished, a secret interview with the king turned the scale in his favour. The Councillor Marillac, with whom Marie was leagued, was arrested and beheaded, and she herself was put under arrest. The choice of a place of exile being allowed her, she selected the Château de Compiègne. All her servants were sent to the Bastille. The plot of Gaston d'Orleans, the king's brother, to excite a civil war for the expulsion of Richelieu was also discovered, and his partizans declared guilty of

* This epithet was applied to it by Maréchal Bassompierre, whose rather *lâche* desertion of De Richelieu, on this occasion, cost him twelve years' confinement in the Bastille, where he wrote his Mémoires.

treason. The brave Duc de Montmorenci was taken prisoner, and by the cardinal's order beheaded at Toulouse.*

The queen-mother, fearing that Vincennes or the Bastille might be her own ultimate destination, escaped from Compiègne and fled to Brussels, where she was at first kindly received and entertained. Paris, which she had adorned with works of art, and which was indebted to her for others of public utility, she was destined to see no more. A stronger hand than Louis's now held the reins of government. Yet the king sanctioned the severities of his minister towards his mother. He was glad to be freed from her domineering influence, but he had no love for Richelieu, and was soon jealous of his power, jealous of the state and splendour with which he surrounded himself; for the cardinal far excelled the sovereign in outward pomp, in the richness of his equipages and the expensiveness of his establishment. Louis felt the bondage he was held in, but feeble in constitution and mentally weak, he was unable to break from the control of the master mind that governed both him and his kingdom.

Richelieu was created a duke, and the king

* The king declined to accept his confiscated estate of Chantilly. He gave the château, parks and grounds to the duke's sister, Charlotte de Montmorenci, Princesse de Condé, and thus this fine domain passed into the Condé family.

gave him the government of Brittany. But the royal authority was a mere shadow to his. He humbled the haughty nobles, extinguished the liberties of the people, and oppressed the Huguenots. The nation groaned under its heavy burden of taxation, and trembled before its sanguinary administrator.

Poor Marie de Médicis, a wandering exile, without money or friends, dependent on the benevolence of foreigners for shelter and subsistence, though she had never in her day of power and prosperity been very popular, now excited the sympathy and compassion of the people as an oppressed queen, an unhappy and injured mother.

CHAPTER VIII.

Richelieu's Patronage of Literature. — Richelieu, Chapelain, and "Le Cid." — The Rambouillet Circle. — Its Discordant Elements. — Social Savoir-faire of the Marquise. — Depravity of the Court. — The Queen and Madame de Hautefort. — Richelieu and Anne of Austria. — Mademoiselle de La Fayette. — Louis XIII. as a Lover. — An Evening at Rambouillet. — The Fiery Calprenède. — " Le Grand Epistolier." — Cardinal de la Valette. — Eaves-dropping. — " Tel Maitre, tel Valet." — Gaston d'Orleans.

HE period which French writers have named "*le grand siècle littéraire*" began with the accession of Cardinal de Richelieu to power. The government of the kingdom with uncontrolled absolute authority was entirely in his hands, and no sort of fame was indifferent to him. The patronage he accorded to literature resulted from no enlightened sympathy with men of letters and their pursuits, but from an undeviating practice of seeking his own exaltation by any and every means that presented itself. To become the recognized patron of men of learning, and especially of the poets, was to enhance his glory while living and to hand down his name to posterity surrounded by a halo of laudatory verse.

But the poets most favoured by Richelieu were those who, of the numerous verse-writers of that day, are now even by name scarcely known, and whose works generally have been consigned to oblivion. Richelieu himself made verses, as a distraction from the heavy cares of state, and pretended to a high, if not the highest, place amongst his poets and *gens de lettres*. But he could brook no rivals near his throne; and as in the government of the kingdom he sent to the Bastille, or the scaffold, all who were obnoxious to him or were obstacles in his path, so in the world of letters he trampled on genius in order to exalt mediocrity in the shape of dramas concocted by himself and his staff of versifiers for representation at the theatre of his own palace.

Jean Chapelain — one of those critics who fail in literature — first obtained favour and temporary fame, and became, as Boileau said, "*le mieux renté de tous les beaux esprits*," by an ode addressed "À son Éminence le Cardinal de Richelieu," and a critique on "Le Cid" of le grand Corneille. This chef-d'œuvre of a great genius displeased His Éminence. To depreciate it was a delicate piece of flattery that met with its certain reward. The great cardinal, like many other so-called great men, had vulnerable points open to successful attack from very poor creatures.

The Hôtel de Rambouillet was more impartial in its judgments, and its voice was a powerful one.

Its circle was now greatly extended; not only the celebrated *salon bleu*, which was especially devoted to the reading of new works and conversations on stated subjects, was overflowing with guests, but its spacious neighbour and rival in elegance, the *salon jaune*, and often the whole suite of reception-rooms, was thrown open to them; so numerously were the *réunions* of the marquise attended. And it was not exclusively a literary coterie, though the *élite* of the *gens de lettres* were present, and obscurely-born genius and rising talent sought and received their welcome and encouragement. Courtiers and ladies of the highest rank, who could make no pretensions to learning and very little to *esprit*, mingled with the throng; attracted by the polished ease and general tone of good-breeding that prevailed in the crowded *salons* of Rambouillet, and contrasted so strikingly with the roughness and grossness of the manners of the court.

It was not necessary to produce quarterings of nobility to obtain an introduction to the assemblies of the marquise; but intelligence, talent, and above all good manners, were indispensable qualifications for that honour. Merit, there, ranked above birth; *esprit* in itself was reckoned a dignity, and to literature and its professors was accorded a degree of consideration which hitherto the grandees of society had rarely, if ever, vouchsafed to them. The Hôtel de Rambouillet served also as a school of manners for the court. The tone of refinement it was necessary to observe there was a protest against the open depravity, both of conduct and speech, which survived in the society of the Louvre, long after the evil example of Henry IV. had ceased to give sanction to it.

The *salons* of Rambouillet afforded, no doubt, many examples of high-flown sentimentality and affectation, as well as of overstrained or stilted politeness. And it has been suspected that before the period of its greatest vogue and importance (from 1635 to 1645) there existed amongst the society that frequented the hôtel, composed as it was of persons of such different social grades, a carefully suppressed undercurrent of mutual disdain. The pride of birth, the pride of intellect, the pride of purse, each received a shock from the presence of the others, and could not immediately amalgamate, though represented there only by the *élite* of each class. It argues in the hostess the possession of a high degree of tact and social *savoir-faire* to have succeeded so happily in soothing the ruffled spirits of her high and mighty guests, and bringing the discordant elements in her circle to act so favourably on each other as to produce that general tone of good breeding, that courtesy of manner, that suavity of expression — indicating respect for others as well as self-respect — which characterized those who had mixed with the *société polie* of Rambouillet.

From Rambouillet emanated "*le sentiment de toutes les bienséances*," and a tone of refinement which, with the spread of the social instinct, gradually imbued French society generally. It is one of the glories of that celebrated hôtel that its influence on the manners of the age was felt by all classes and conditions, even to the inferior degrees of the social scale, and has never, through all the changing fortunes of the nation, become wholly extinct. If no great amendment was wrought by its influence on the morals of the age, at least the attempt to reform them was made by inculcating a respect for purity of life, of which the unblemished one of the marquise afforded an example. For a full century — from the time of Francis I. to the end of the reign of Henry IV. — the court (and there was no other society) had been deeply plunged in vice. The regency of Marie de Médicis produced no improvement — though no well-substantiated charge of immorality has been brought against *her*. Richelieu's private life was far from blameless, and though Louis XIII. did not pursue a depraved career, like his father and his son, his example had no weight whatever, because of his gloomy seclusion, his stern neglect of his wife, his harsh, perhaps unjust suspicions of her, and their mutual indifference, if not actual dislike.

Louis had read "Astrée," and had adopted

D'Urfé's system of "*honnête amitié.*" Madame de Hautefort, afterwards Duchesse de Schomberg, but who was then one of the queen's *dames d'honneur*, was the object of this tenderly respectful flame, after the Duchesse de Luynes became Duchesse de Chévreuse. Madame de Hautefort was much attached to the queen, and the two ladies seem to have amused themselves greatly at the expense of the king. It was his custom to go daily to the gallery of the Louvre, where the queen and her ladies assemble to chatter and laugh and amuse themselves; for Anne was both desperately ignorant and indolent. She delighted in petty intrigue, and her *laissez-aller* disposition saved her from many mortifications. Louis took no notice whatever of his wife, but sat down at some distance from the group and gazed long and sadly on Madame de Hautefort. The queen, after a time, would bid her "go and talk to him for pity's sake," when he would draw her aside, or beckon her into the deep recess of some window, and there tell her of his amusements; either of the chase, or of his gardening, and carpentering — for he excelled in these occupations. He was also a good barber, and had recently practised on the gentlemen of his household who wore beards, leaving them only a small tuft of hair on the centre of the chin. This became, and still is, as we all know, a fashion in France; the tuft of hair, in compliment to the royal barber, being called "*la royale.*" *

When these subjects failed, he descanted on the politics of the day, or told his fair *bergère* how many Huguenots his army, by the help of Heaven, had slain. The influence of Madame de Hautefort was very great with the king, but he inspired in her no feeling beyond pity. Ultimately, in her endeavours to serve the queen, she became suspected by the cardinal, and was banished from the court. For Richelieu delighted to humiliate Anne of Austria, because of her haughty rejection of the loverlike advances he had presumed to make towards her, and Madame de Hautefort, as he was aware, had greatly aided her to escape the consequences of her share in a plot or secret correspondence with Spain.

The king did not immediately reconcile himself to the loss of the society of Madame de Hautefort, but the wily cardinal contrived to throw in his way a far more sympathetic young lady—Mademoiselle de La Fayette. She appears to have been really interested in Louis, and even

---

* This fancy of the king produced several chansonnettes which were sung in the streets; the gentlemen who had undergone the operation being often saluted with:

"Hélas! ma pauvre barbe,
Qu'es qui t'a faite ainsi?
C'est le grand roi, Louis,
Troisième de ce nom,
Qui toute a ébarbé sa maison," etc., etc.

to have felt for him a very warm attachment.
He, who is said never to have felt either friendship or love for any one, or to have regarded
his greatest favourites as anything more to him
than slaves created to contribute to his pleasures
and amusements, managed to infuse into this
new *liaison* a large dash of sentiment. So much,
indeed, that momentarily forgetful of the D'Urfé
principles upon which he so piqued himself, he
proposed to Mademoiselle de La Fayette to share
with him his château of St. Germain, that they
might there live for each other alone.

La belle demoiselle was alarmed, and resolved
to seek refuge in a convent from the friend who
had become her lover. His entreaties prevailed
not to shake her resolution, and Vincent de Paul,
who was the king's spiritual director, used every
argument to confirm her in it. Fearing ill consequences from delay, he urged on her the
necessity of at once acting on her resolve, and
obtained permission to conduct her himself to
the Carmelites. There Louis visited her; for
convent gates were not closed to the kings of
France. It was their royal prerogative to enter
any of the religious houses whenever they would.
And Louis availed himself of it to talk to the
fair penitent for hours together of politics and
affairs of state. She had fled from a phantom.
The proposal at which virtue took alarm, was
uttered under the influence of a feeling that

passed away when the words that gave expression to it were spoken. But lest there should be any revival, Father Vincent kept a vigilant eye on the sentimental friends. He remonstrated, too, with the king on the scandal likely to arise from his passing so much of his time in a nunnery; and at length he prevailed on Mademoiselle de La Fayette, still in her novitiate, to refuse to receive his visits, and to delay not her full profession as a nun.

When, in 1631, Marie de Médicis was finally banished from the court, many of the *fêtes* and other gaieties she had introduced there were banished also. The *tristesse* that ensued caused a great influx of new visitors at the Hôtel de Rambouillet. There the *grands seigneurs* and *grandes dames*, though they found fewer noisy amusements and less boisterous mirth, yet met with new subjects of interest. And as novelty is always attractive, the court was almost deserted, except by those whose attendance was obligatory.

It was a warm evening in the genial month of May. The wide doors that separated the suite of *salons* were removed from their hinges; the long windows thrown open. Outside each of them was a large basketful of sweet-scented flowers, placed on a low stand. Some of the company, allured by the beauty of the evening, were promenading in the garden. A numerous circle had assembled in the one vast saloon, as it then appeared to be; the Venetian mirrors at either end reflecting, and repeating the reflexion, *ad infinitum*, of the lighted lamps and the moving groups of guests. Jean Louis Balzac was there, and Chapelain — he was considered an oracle, then; alas for his reputation, that he published those first six books of his terrible "Pucelle." There was Pierre Corneille — no "Cid," as yet — and young Gaultier de la Calprenède, just venturing to try his skill in a long romance after the D'Urfé fashion. Calprenède was "*un gentilhomme de l'antichambre du roi*" — a Gascon, fiery and impetuous, with his hand ever on his sword-hilt, ready at any hour to unsheathe his weapon and to defend his works *à toute outrance*.

Calprenède had written a short dramatic piece which had been submitted to His Eminence, who had greatly dispraised it, and said that the least of its faults was that it was written in "*vers lâches.*" At the word "*lâches*" Calprenède fired up, as if at a personal insult. "*Cadédis!*" he exclaimed, clapping his hand on his sword, "*comment lâches? il n'y a jamais eu rien de lâche dans la maison de la Calprenède!*" His Eminence did not, as might have been expected, reply "Off with his head," as he would willingly have done to another Buckingham, who, like himself, had ventured to look with eyes of loving admiration on the pious coquette, Anne of Austria.

But to return to the *salon bleu*. A learned conversation was going on, in which Balzac was the chief speaker. He was arguing for the adoption into the French language of the word *urbanité*. It was not then French; and, indeed, the thing signified had until lately been almost a stranger in the land. But it had found a home at Rambouillet, and it was just and fit that its naturalization in France should be accomplished there by its sanction of the word best suited to describe it.

Jean Louis Balzac was eloquent, both as a writer and speaker, but in a style too sonorous, too Johnsonian. Some one has irreverently spoken of it, as "*la langue française à la torture.*" His early correspondence with Madame de Rambouillet, on the Romans and their history, is in a high degree stilted and inflated. But Balzac had become sensible of this defect, and resolved to correct it. Prose writers who used the mother tongue were few: consequently there were no approved French models to form a style upon. Idyls, sonnets, and odes; chansons, and chansonnettes, and short versified *pièces de théâtre*, sufficed to make a literary reputation; and in them the witty and epigrammatic spirit of the nation was clearly enough apparent, but not the force and beauty of the language. Very few, indeed, were thoroughly acquainted with it. Amongst these few Balzac, "*le grand épistolier*," was chief. He had secluded himself for some years, and devoted them exclusively to the study of language and the improvement of his style. The purity and elegance with which the French tongue was spoken and written later on in the seventeenth century are in a great measure due to Balzac. He was also the first who excelled in epistolary writing.

The literary men assembled at this date (1631) in the *salons* of Rambouillet are all young — Balzac, who is thirty-nine, is a veteran amongst them.* Only the historian Vaugelas is his senior; unless the great cardinal's poet and humble servant, Boisrobert, be honoured with a place among *les gens de lettres*. Boisrobert was at the hôtel, on the occasion above referred to, in the quality of political spy. He was commissioned to keep a watchful eye on all that was done, and an open ear to all that was said by Madame la Princesse de Condé (sister of the Duke de Montmorenci) and the Cardinal de la Valette, Richelieu's brother, and like himself a soldier-priest. La princesse, in a cosy arm-chair, and well out of earshot of the learned conversation of the *littérateurs* and *les dames savantes*, is in close confidential confabulation with the cardinal, who is seated on a low

---

* The old poet Malherbe had died three years before, and Ogier de Gombauld, whose pension of 1200 écus was reduced to 400 francs, did not often appear. The marquise frequently and anonymously relieved his distress, and furnished him with respectable clothing for his occasional visits.

stool, drawn up very close to the arm-chair of the princess.

(It may be observed here, *en passant*, that the cardinal is the recognized "*honnête homme*" of Madame la Princesse, according to the rules of the establishment, to be referred to by-and-by.)

Most provokingly, Boisrobert sees that much is being said, but not a syllable reaches his ear; and he is too well-known to venture to approach and dexterously to glide into or interrupt the conversation. The buzz and the hum of voices around Balzac, the occasional ting-tang of a lute in the music room, and the twittering of that pretty spinnet, are all in league with these earnest talkers, whose *confidences* at last come to an end with a laugh that to Boisrobert's ears has a derisive sound, but makes him no wiser as to the subject of the discourse. This he reported to his master, who forthwith despatched the wily Père Josephe, to say to the marquise that His Eminence suspected his brother and Madame la Princesse of carrying on intrigues with the Spanish Court, where the Marquis de Rambouillet was then ambassador, and that he desired, therefore, to know all that was said by them in her *salon* on the subject of Spanish affairs.

The marquise replied, "she did not believe that Cardinal de la Valette and the princess were engaged in any intrigues on the subject; but, if they were, that His Eminence must excuse her from playing the part of spy on those who frequented her *salons*."

Richelieu had already deprived Rambouillet of one of the most lively of its *preux chevaliers*— the Maréchal de Bassompierre, who had too prematurely rejoiced over the supposed downfall of the minister. Le maréchal's courtly and chivalric devotion to the fair sex had made Bassompierre and gallantry almost synonymous terms. His valet, who had lived with him many years, aspired to similar renown, and had fully established his reputation as a squire of dames; the proverb "*Tel maître, tel valet*," is said to have been first applied to this gallant knight and his trusty squire. Vincent Voiture was another absentee. When in Paris, he lived so constantly at the Hôtel de Rambouillet, that he was familiarly called "Voiture de l'Hôtel." He was attached to the household of Gaston d'Orléans, the king's brother, who was then in Lorraine, having failed in his plots against the cardinal, and abandoned his friends, who now suffered for his pusillanimity.

Gaston was the father of the celebrated Grande Mademoiselle. At this time she was about five years of age. Her mother, who had died in giving birth to her, was the beautiful Mademoiselle de Montpensier, heiress to the immense wealth of the House of Guise, and also allied to the crown. Louis XIII., though he had neither affection nor respect for Anne of Austria, was extraordinarily jealous of any attentions that were paid to her, even by his boy-brother, whom he hated. He suspected them of conspiring together to dethrone him, with a view of then marrying and usurping his authority. Gaston was therefore compelled to take a wife; and, much against his will, married the young and beautiful bride Louis found for him. She died the following year. Gaston afterwards married one of the princesses of the house of Lorraine; pleasing himself in his second marriage, and thereby sorely displeasing the king.

CHAPTER IX.

Boisrobert. — M. le Prince. — The Mysterious Oublieuse. —Her Lute and her Song. — La Belle Angélique Paulet. — Her Music and Dancing. — The Jealous Nightingales. — A Presumptuous Bourgeois. — Patriotism, Religion, and Love. — A Noble Lover. — Galants et Honnêtes Hommes. — Social Supremacy of Woman.

THE great cardinal, after 1630, no longer frequented the *salons* where so many were welcomed whom he regarded either as his literary rivals or political foes. Had he ventured to do so, he would have met there also, in the course of the next few years, some bitter personal enemies in the representatives of those families, several of whose members had been sent by him to the scaffold. His favourite and secretary, as well as literary *protégé*, Boisrobert — a man of some wit and much pleasantry, and who was also fond of the society of men of letters — kept a watchful eye open on the company for him. Madame la Princesse he now suspected of intriguing with Spain; a few years later on, he knew that she abhorred the man whom she regarded as the murderer of her brother, Montmorenci. But the enmity of Monsieur le Prince — who, though extremely wealthy, was extremely parsimonious and avaricious — was greatly modified by the gift of his brother-in-law's confiscated estate of Chantilly. His three years' sojourn at Vincennes had also had a subduing effect both on his resentment and his courage.

Richelieu had no persistent enemy in him. But even then, 1631, he desired to repress the mutinous spirit, and to alienate from the court the youth who stood beside the Prince de Condé listening to Balzac. This youth of eighteen was the Prince de Marsillac (de La Rochefoucauld of "Les Maximes"). Like many others of the company who did not join in the conversation of the literary circle, they had been drawn away from it by the sound of music, which now and then reached them faintly from a distance, yet not from the music-room. It was the sound of a lute, very skilfully played.

The performer was a woman. She stood outside the open window at the extreme end of the suite of *salons*. The dense foliage of a large tree threw a deep shadow over her, and she seemed to avoid every flickering ray of light which, as the guests from time to time moved, fell on the pathway from the lamps of the *salons*. "*C'est une oublieuse*," said one of the ladies, as the woman approached the window, and, curtseying gracefully, placed before the audience her music had drawn thither a large Flemish basket, decorated with red ribands, and filled with wafer-cakes, or *oubliettes*, then hastily drew back. Curiosity was piqued. The night was clear and starlight, and it was perceived that although her dress was of the fashion of the class she represented, like her basket, it was unusually natty and coquettish.

The short linen petticoat was looped up with red ribands and very jaunty bows; her "*calle*," or coif, which was rather ample, as if for concealment, was also bordered and tied with ribands of the same colour. She was neither barefooted nor shod with heavy *sabots*, but wore coloured stockings with elaborately-worked clocks, and pretty shoes, with the bands, bows, and heels *à la* Louis Treize, or as they should rather be called, *à la* Anne d'Autriche, as she introduced them from Spain.

"*Dieu! quelle jolie main blanche et potelée!*" said young Marsillac, as the mysterious "*oublieuse*" struck a full chord with a firm and practised hand, and played the air of a *chanson* by Malherbe, then greatly in vogue.

"Why not sing it?" said Julie d'Angennes. "It is one of Angélique Paulet's favourite songs. I must ask mamma," she continued, "who this stranger woman is."

Madame de Rambouillet protested she did not know, and that inquiry must be made how she got into the grounds.

"*C'est une laideron*," said Monsieur le Prince, "or she'd show us her face."

"*Peut-être une empoisonneuse*," whispered another to a little group of ladies who were admiring the Flemish basket and eating the *oubliettes*.

This remark caused some commotion, so general was the dread and suspicion of poison in those days. But all this time the lute went ting-tang, ting-tang, merrily on. At the word "poison" a little low laugh seemed to issue from the coif, and the mysterious personage stepped forward, drew back her basket, and placed it by her side. Again she struck her lute, and began the same air; but there was a general demand for the words. Nothing daunted, she advanced more directly in front of the window, as if to face her audience, preluded a little, then began her song in a rich, full, sweet voice, that sympathetically thrilled through every auditor. "*Mais, c'est Angélique! c'est Angélique!*" was the general exclamation. The coif of the *oblieuse* fell, and revealed Mademoiselle Paulet to her friends and admirers.*

"When that great king," says Mademoiselle de Scudéry, speaking of Henry IV., "gave what he called his heart to any *belle fille* of the queen's court, it was always injurious to her reputation." And so it proved to Angélique Paulet's, though

---

* This is not an imaginary scene. It took place at the Hôtel de Rambouillet. Mademoiselle Paulet appears to have been fond of assuming these disguises, and to have introduced the practice amongst the ladies of Rambouillet.

when Henry's last visit was paid to Angélique on the morning of his death, she was but in her seventeenth year. Her father is said to have been by no means unwilling to obtain lucrative and responsible posts through the favour enjoyed by his daughter, while her mother, a handsome woman of low birth, who died shortly before the assassination of the king, was so constantly engaged in intrigue, that she entirely neglected her, and gave her over from childhood to the charge of servants.

Angélique at an early age became an orphan, with a disputed inheritance, of which the laws (then in a most unsatisfactory state) gave her only a portion, after some years of litigation. Madame de Rambouillet had had a great regard for her as a young girl, and desired to welcome her to her hôtel; but the blemish on her reputation must first be effaced, and "*il fallait*," says a French writer, "*du temps pour la laisser purger.*" During that time she resided with the Comtesse de Clermont d'Entragues, a woman of great distinction and very high character. Under her auspices Mademoiselle Paulet was received at the Hôtel de Rambouillet.

She excelled in dancing — the fashionable accomplishment of the day — and as a vocalist and skilful performer on the théorbe and lute she had no rival. Music was scarcely studied at all in France at that time, and Angélique's simple airs, sung with natural taste, and a full, sweet voice, no doubt enraptured her hearers. There must have been some real charm in those exquisite notes that held her listeners spellbound. The poetic anecdote invented to convey an idea of their beauty seems to bear evidence of it. She is said to have been singing to her lute in a part of the gardens frequented by nightingales, and that two of these feathered songsters left the trees and perched on the edge of a fountain to listen. As she continued warbling on, now in a full, rich strain, now soft, subdued, and tender, the listening birds strove at times to emulate her tuneful ditty. In vain, in vain, — their heavenly gift of song is gone. Still they listen, jealous, despairing, yet entranced. But when the sweet strain ceased, the nightingales drooped and died!

So highly was she esteemed at Rambouillet, that on the occasion of her first visit to the Hôtel the marquise sent a troop of the prettiest girls of the place, as well as those of her own household, to meet her at her entrance on the Rambouillet domain. Their dresses were wreathed with flowers, and one of the girls, selected as the prettiest, carried an ornamented basket, containing the keys of the *château*. These, on bended knee, she presented to the much-honoured visitor, who, as she passed over the drawbridge, was saluted also by the firing of the two small cannon. She is described as exceedingly pretty, with a brilliant complexion, golden hair, and graceful figure. In the little drawing-room dramas that were performed at Rambouillet, either in a small theatre or fitted-up *salon*, Mademoiselle Paulet — dressed as a nymph — was accustomed to dance and sing between the acts. This performance being substituted for "the usual interlude of the hired violins."

Angélique was no longer in her *première jeunesse*. In 1631 she was full thirty-seven. Tallemant des Réaux, a constant frequenter of Rambouillet, says she was called "*la lionne, à cause de ses yeux vifs, ses cheveux roux, sa fierté et courage.*" He adds that the prudery of this lioness was excessive, insupportable; and that some three years before she shook her mane violently, and roared with anger when a rich *marchand linger* of the neighbourhood presumed to fall in love with her, and to hire a band of serenaders to sing *chansonnettes amoureuses*, and to play the lute and violin beneath her windows. The presumption *de cet animal là*, when, on the return of the king from the siege of Rochelle (the *marchand* was "*capitaine de son quartier*"), he drew up his men, all decked with green ribands — green being a colour affected by the fair one — and saluted her with a salvo of musketry, excited her boundless indignation.

But the fair Angélique was compelled to

smooth her brow, and if not to smile graciously on the gallant *marchand linger*, at least not to frown very much upon him. For it came into his mind to celebrate the cardinal's triumph at Rochelle by a *fête*, at which he prayed all the wealthy and great of his *quartier* to condescend to assist. He possessed a good house, with a fine garden; was decidedly a man of substance, and doubtless of some influence, though the historian of the Hôtel de Rambouillet does not give his name. At all events the marquise approved his idea, and with her daughter and some of the ladies of her society — amongst them Mademoiselle Paulet — condescendingly graced the festive scene with her presence.

In thus honouring a rich linendraper, the marquise, in her quality of *grande dame*, believed that she encouraged in persons of his class the patriotic fervour and religious enthusiasm at the discomfiture of the Huguenots of Rochelle, of which her *protégé* seemed to set so praiseworthy an example. But *les beaux yeux* of Mademoiselle Paulet on this occasion influenced the gallant *bourgeois* far more potently than either patriotism or religious zeal. She was the queen to whom he would willingly have sworn fealty; she was the goddess at whose shrine he would have worshipped. But his ardent loyalty and devotion, poor fellow, received a check, and it is to be hoped an effectual cure, in the scorn with which they were repelled.

Had not a king sighed for Mademoiselle Angélique? Had not two princes of Lorraine worn her chains? One, indeed — the Duc de Chévreuse — had half ruined himself in the purchase of diamonds and pearls of great price for the adornment of charms that needed no fictitious aids to enhance them. But the lady was not, it appears, duly affected by the munificence of this lover. Much annoyed, and repenting of his lavish expenditure, he determined to repossess himself of the jewels, which were enclosed in a richly ornamented casket. He did not request their return, but hearing that she had for some reason confided them, until the proceedings respecting her property were concluded, to the care of a person named Decoudrais, the prince employed a man in his service to abstract them; and he succeeded in doing so, probably with the connivance of the friend into whose charge they were given. But Mademoiselle Paulet had yet a numerous train of lovers — "*amants inoffensifs*," a contemporary writer calls them — and the chief of them was *le bel esprit*, Vincent Voiture.

In the Rambouillet society, every gentleman was bound to be the lover, or *galant et honnête homme*, of one or other of the ladies. He was to be the devoted slave of his mistress — something after the manner of the knights of the heroic age, combined with the sentimentality of the Strephons and Florimels of D'Urfé and Calprenède, though with more punctiliousness than the swains of the Gascon romancer affected in their social relations with their nymphs. He must blend with knightly honour and gallantry the simplicity of Arcadia and the courtesy of high breeding, while the lady of whom he was the humble servant and respectful adorer graciously tempered the stateliness of a high-born Mandane with a dash of the tenderness of a Phyllis.

Manners so constrained and artificial as to appear utterly ludicrous were, however, but a protest against the extreme laxity and grossness of the court, and the thorough demoralization of society produced by its example — just as the ignorance of the illiterate *grands seigneurs* was reproved by the reception at Rambouillet — *pair à pair* with the first nobles of the land — of the *gens de lettres* they were inclined to contemn. And they were received with even greater distinction, for no patronage or influence could purchase a welcome for them; their talents, learning and wit were the titles that procured them respect. "*Les grands*," says Roederer, "*s'étonnèrent un moment de cette égalité; mais ils s'y firent.*"

It is probable that for some time the literary element, with its learned conversations and discussions, contributed more towards the improvement of the French language than the refinement of manners; for the poets and men of letters sprang for the most part from the ranks of the people, or from the *bourgeoisie*, who availed themselves of the opportunities the collegiate schools afforded to studiously-disposed youths of acquiring learning. Roughnesses, however, would soon be toned down in that stately society, and wit and genius, with their odes, their idyls, and epistles to the ladies, aid in establishing the social supremacy of woman in France — first achieved at the Hôtel de Rambouillet, and still so generally maintained.

CHAPTER X.

The Urbanity Question. — Printed Discourses and News-Letters. — The *Mercure* and *Gazette de France*. — Romances of D'Urfé and Calprenède. — A Rival in the Field. — Madeleine de Scudéry. — Georges de Scudéry. — Julie d'Angennes. — Madeleine at Rambouillet. — Madeleine as a Poetess. — The Plays of Georges de Scudéry. — Georges a Virtuoso. — An Address to the Gentle Reader. — Success of " Le Prince Déguisé." — Georges popular at Rambouillet.

THE "urbanity question," like many of a similar nature discussed at Rambouillet, was considered an important one. The conversation respecting it ended in a unanimous vote that "*urbanité* take a permanent place in the French vocabulary." The pros and the cons were noted down; for as the literary part of the Rambouillet circle had not assembled in full force that evening, a *résumé* of the discussion was required for the absent members. Sometimes, when the subject discussed was of unusual interest, the conversations upon it were printed, and forwarded to those friends and acquaintances who resided mostly at their provincial *châteaux*. In this habit of reporting the conversations of the *salons*, literary or otherwise, originated many of those epistolary writings of the seventeenth century since collected and published. They were the conversations of parted friends and relations — the interchange of opinions on topics of interest and the passing events of the day, of which no information would have reached the provinces but for the facile pens of diligent letter-writers.

And very welcome those printed discourses and budgets of news must have been in those days of literary famine and undeveloped newspaper press; far more so than is now the arrival of a box of new books from Mudie's at a dull country house, empty of guests, and on a rainy day. There were no magazines even then, except those that contained the state's powder. No daily or weekly chronicle of the follies, the vices, the crimes, the amusements, the miseries of all grades of society all the world over; no Wednesday, Friday or Saturday reviews, to give the idle and busy the pith of a big book in a nut-shell, and save them the trouble of reading and of forming opinions for themselves; no *Gazette of Fashion* and *World of Elegance* to describe to *les dames provinciales* the latest *modes parisiennes;* in fact, none of the present thousand and one vehicles of good, bad and indifferent literary food, and few — very few — of the amusements, distractions, and so-called pleasures of life that to so many make life now scarcely endurable.

There was Renaudot's *Mercure* and there was the *Gazette de France,* for which Louis himself wrote bulletins of the war; for a war, either foreign or civil and religious, was always on hand, and frequently both. But these puny sheets contained no court circular; no births, marriages and deaths; no agony column; no "fashionable intelligence" of marriages on the *tapis*, or marriages dissolved; of the comings and goings of the *haute volée* to their places and mansions in country or town, or for runs round the world; no lists of the shoals of inmates filling the marine mansions and grand hotels; none, indeed, of the innumerable trivialities concerning the world's doings in general, and which are now fully chronicled for the particular edification of those who deem it necessary and important to be duly and correctly informed of them.

With none of these resources of the present day to fall back upon for small talk, the discussions of the Hôtel de Rambouillet on language, or on the merits of a new book, formed themes of conversation both instructive and interesting for those families who, from political or economical motives, rarely visited the capital; and thus, though residing at a distance from it, they shared in some degree the advantages of those who formed part of that *société d'élite*, as well as helped to further its principal objects — the perfecting of the French tongue, the spreading of a taste for polite literature, and the cultivation of refinement of manners, as a first step towards an improvement in the morals of the age.

In this way D'Urfé's fame was, as it were, advertised and spread far and wide; and still more so that of his successor, Calprenède, who, though keeping on the borders of Arcadia, contrived to endow his heroes with a more chivalric spirit than those of D'Urfé. His impetuous knights, distressed princesses in disguise, sighing swains, and faithless fair ones, pass through a series of adventures truly astonishing. But, extravagant as they are, Calprenède brings all his personages well through their troubles; some, perhaps, when their worst trials beset them, are reduced to such straits by their constancy and heroism, that, with Francis I. (who had no honour to lose), they might triumphantly exclaim, "*Tout est perdu sauf l'honneur!*"

Calprenède's eight quarto volume romances met with the most signal success. They found a welcome in every *château* in the kingdom, and were read with avidity. Edition succeeded edition, until the author could satisfy the eager demand of both town and country readers for another long history of the sentimental gallantries of shepherd life, and imaginary feats of chivalry. The ludicrous improbability of his stories seems to have been no bar to their popularity. It may, indeed, have been one cause of it, for the Gascon romancer was reproached only for brevity. Yet each of his volumes, of eight hundred to a thousand well-filled pages, contained not less than six of the modern three-hundred-paged volumes. They were published singly, as they were written — one or two in the course of a year — and as they abounded in episodes, romance within romance, a great fault in itself, yet suspense was not so agonizing as if the whole interest of the work had been centred in two or three of its characters. But a rival of more cultured mind, more fertile brain, and less extravagant fancy, and who held a more facile pen, was shortly to eclipse the fame of Calprenède; this rival was Madeleine de Scudéry.

Amongst the ladies who frequented the Hôtel de Rambouillet, none, in her day, attained greater literary celebrity than Mademoiselle de Scudéry. Born in 1607, she lived to 1701, nearly a whole century, entering very early on a literary career, and pursuing it until quite an advanced age. Many of the changes which occurred in the language during that period, in its orthography, in the adoption of certain forms of expression and the rejection of others were either originated by her, or owed their reception to her sanction or her use of them. If it be permitted to employ the term "representative women," Mademoiselle de Scudéry of all contemporary female writers has the strongest claim, both from her length of years and the number and success of her works, to be named the representative of the polite literature of the seventeenth century, as approved at Rambouillet.

The Hôtel de Rambouillet was then more of a court than the Louvre. Not to be received there was equivalent to being outside the pale of good society. Introductions to the marquise were anxiously sought for. To have but once spent an evening in the famous *salon bleu* amongst the *beaux esprits*, the *littérateurs*, the rank and fashion, the wealth and beauty of the capital, was to have achieved an envied social distinction. To obtain it was an inducement to gifted youth, poor in purse and lowly born, to persevere in the acquirement of learning, of artistic skill, or excellence in whatever branch of literature or the arts they might be pursuing.

Madeleine de Scudéry and her brother Georges, who was six years her senior, first visited Rambouillet in 1622, at the special invitation of the marquise. Georges was then twenty-one, and a lieutenant of the Gardes du Roi,—Madeleine but fifteen. Both were already known for their poetical talents. Left orphans at an early age, they had been brought up by a maternal uncle, who gave Madeleine the same education as her brother; Latin and Greek forming part of their studies. Notwithstanding his six years' seniority, Georges had acquired less of the dead languages than his sister, who was far more studiously inclined. She was an eager reader of romances, of works on theology, on agriculture, or any subject, in fact, that her uncle's miscellaneous collection of books gave her an opportunity of obtaining a knowledge of. This uncle seems to have been a good sort of genial old bachelor. Not rich, but living thoroughly at his ease in Paris; enjoying the company of the *beaux esprits*, doing his best for his adopted children, rather spoiling little Madeleine, whose vivacity and *espièglerie* amused him, and at his death leaving his small property to them.

Georges and Madeleine were both born at Havre, where their parents had settled, though they were of a good old Provençal family. Madeleine, on the death of her uncle, found a protectress in Madame de Rambouillet. Amiable in disposition, full of talent, well educated, well born, well bred, but scantily provided for, the Marquise thought Madeleine de Scudéry a desirable companion for her eldest daughter Julie. The young girls were of nearly the same age, and became greatly attached to each other. Some writers have described Julie as "*excessivement jolie*," others have dwelt upon her mental gifts and pleasing manners. But *jolie* was not usually employed in the seventeenth century to express beauty of person; it meant something more, and, as applied to Julie d'Angennes, that she was a charming girl, though probably not regularly beautiful.

Of Madeleine de Scudéry we are told more precisely, "*qu'elle possédait toutes les charmes, sauf celle de la beauté physique.*" Poor girl, she had been robbed of her beauty by that terrible scourge of those days — smallpox. Happily she was not of sufficient consideration in the world to be obliged to hide her scarred features in a convent, and fritter away her great mental gifts in the debasing pettinesses of the purposeless life of a cloistered nun. Madeleine was not exactly domiciled at the Hôtel de Rambouillet, though she passed much of her time there. She noted down the conversations on the various subjects proposed for discussion; not in the exact words of the speakers, but rather as a condensed report of their opinions and the result arrived at, — for they were written after the conversation had closed. Only by sustained attention and an excellent memory could she have accomplished her task. And no doubt to this frequent exercise of both were owing that ease and ability with which, when in after years she wrote ten-volume romances, the long conversations of her characters were carried on. Dialogue was one of her chief excellences. The conversations on moral subjects were separated from the works that contained them, and published as models of their kind, and most successfully, long after her death.

But during the period now referred to, 1622 to 1632, Mademoiselle de Scudéry did not write romances. She wrote, as was the fashion with those who had ability, and indeed with many who had not, numberless short pieces of poetry. They are remarkable for delicacy of sentiment, a happy turn of thought, and finish, and correctness in expression that might claim an honourable niche for her amongst the poets of the day. But the fame of her novels entirely eclipsed that of her poems. They were, however, sufficiently appreciated to obtain for her the appellation of Sappho. This became her "*nom de Parnasse*" at Rambouillet, and she was familiarly known and addressed by it to the end of her life. Mademoiselle de Scudéry was one of those charming persons occasionally met with, whose excellent qualities of heart and mind command esteem, and in whom plainness of feature is obliterated by the goodness and intelligence that beam in the countenance and secure admiration denied to mere beauty. For notwithstanding the want of it in her face, her amiability, graceful figure and *distinguée* manners inspired in her youth more than one *grande passion*, and the number of her friends might be reckoned by that of her acquaintances.

Georges de Scudéry, though his fame has been less enduring than his sister's, was by no means deficient in talent. In his day he was regarded as the rival of Corneille, and his plays had immense success. Some portions of "Le Cid" were attributed to his pen, and many parts of his own dramas were considered to possess so much poetic beauty that the author of "Le Cid" might have been proud to acknowledge them. It was never asserted during his life that Corneille assisted Scudéry. But a French writer of more recent date has seemed to imply it in the remark that in Scudéry's verses there is "*un souffle de Corneille.*" It is more than probable that Georges de Scudéry would have rejected the aid of Corneille — for he had a very high opinion of his own abilities. He was as boastful and almost as ready as Calprenède to draw his sword in defence of his works, and to avenge any implied slur on his literary reputation.

That there was more than *un souffle de Madeleine* in them, no one doubted. The jealous Calprenède once asserted that the dedications and prefaces alone belonged to Georges, and these two fiery gentlemen crossed swords in consequence. But it is certain that she greatly assisted him in his literary work. Whatever she wrote herself was published in his name, even when it was fully understood that she was the author. The brother and sister lived together, and she not only corrected his writings but corrected his conduct, and played in many respects the *rôle* of Providence to him. For Georges was a very fine gentleman, a dashing officer of La Garde Royale, with very little money and very expensive tastes.

He collected *virtù*, and had contracted the tulip mania to such a degree that he was content to ruin himself to obtain a scarce bulb. He was fond of pictures, and contrived to get together a gallery of interesting portraits. The talents of his sister he estimated as highly as his own, and compelled her to make diligent use of them. It was his habit to lock her in her study for a certain number of hours daily, allowing no visitors to have access to her. Between them they earned a large sum by the pen, and though Georges spent the income of both, as well as nearly the whole of their literary gains besides his pay as an officer of the Guards, he was never free from debt. Three times Madeleine was on the eve of marriage, but Georges always stepped in and opposed it. In two instances they were desirable matches, advantageous to her in every respect. Her brother's opposition therefore can only be accounted for by crediting him with selfish motives; yet Georges had always the reputation of being a man of the most chivalric sentiments, the very soul of honour, though *un peu fanfaron.* He was supposed to write only for his amusement, and was fond of making this known in prefaces and dedications addressed to "L'Ami Lecteur." In one of these prefaces he says:

"If I write, it is because I have nothing better to do, and my only object in writing is to amuse and please myself. So far from being mercenary, the printers and players will bear me witness that I have not asked them to buy, even when I might have expected them to pay. My gentle readers will readily pass over any faults they detect, which may have escaped me, when they learn that I have spent more years in camps than hours in my study, that I have burnt more matches in firing the arquebuse than in lighting candles, so that I better know how to range soldiers in order of battle than words in their proper places, and to square a battalion than to round a period."

Notwithstanding this affectation of writing for amusement, Georges de Scudéry's literary labour was substantially rewarded, and deservedly so. For his dramatic pieces were highly successful, and excited the envy and rage of Richelieu's company of poets. One of his pieces was played at the cardinal's theatre, and proved more attractive than any that had preceded it. Another, "Le Prince déguisé," was played at the Court Theatre in the Louvre and at several other places. It appears to have had, what was unusual in those days for a short, slight piece of pleasantry, a very long run. Wherever, and however often it was played, all who could obtain admission ran after it. It formed, for a considerable time, the delight of the court. The queen was charmed with it; all Paris talked of it; whole stanzas were often quoted, and at Rambouillet the ladies knew it almost by heart.

No wonder that Georges de Scudéry, who was

so well inclined to mount a high pedestal, should consider that he was justified in the good opinion he entertained of himself by the success he met with, and the reward it brought him; if not in direct payment, in valuable presents, and, what he liked fully as well, an overwhelming amount of flattering compliments. He was a favourite at Rambouillet, where he basked in the sunshine of ladies' smiles as a pleasant scapegrace, a charming fellow. But he had not Chapelain's talent of putting money in his purse and keeping it there. Yet could he have devoted himself to sounding the praises of the great cardinal as much as he delighted to sound his own, he might have acquired places and pensions, and have had money enough and to spare for the full gratification of his expensive horticultural and artistic tastes. It is, however, pleasing to meet with a literary man, who was also a poor one, and who yet could refrain from bowing down and kissing the dust, and offering the incense of flattery before the tyrannical dispenser of court favours.

CHAPTER XI.

The Plague of 1631. — Terror of the People. — Wretched State of the City. — The Château de St. Germain. — A Royal Cook. — The Queen and her Ladies. — Anne and Louis at Thirty Years of Age. — The Rage for Dancing. — Richelieu's ostentatious Pomp. — The Regulation of Costume. — Mortification of the Noblesse. — The Right Divine. — The Plague at Rambouillet. — A Miracle.

IN 1631, Paris — which in the preceding year had been wasted by famine, and desolated by fire that had destroyed the sacristy of the Sainte Chapelle and injured several of its public buildings — was visited by one of those terrible outbreaks of plague, whose fearful ravages during the sixteenth and seventeenth centuries so frequently thinned its population. When it became known that this fatal scourge was again among them, every heart was appalled, and dread of the disease had almost as many victims as the disease itself. How many, trembling for their own lives and the lives of those dearest to them, watched in agony for the first appearance of the dreaded plague-spot in their families! How many, made cruel and heartless by the sight of this supposed sure sign of the grasp of death upon their loved ones, fled — precipitately fled — to escape from it themselves, leaving parents, husband, wife, to sink, uncared for and alone, under the relentless hand of the grim destroyer — *la peste!*

La peste! No word signifying death to the victim of the disease it represents was ever so fraught with terror as this. Stout hearts that would have braved death in any other form quailed before it, and tenderest ones were turned to stone. It was not simply death they feared, but the horrors of *la peste*, the heart-sickening horrors with which imagination invested it as preceding death. The rich and noble generally sought safety in their provincial *châteaux;* some few, trusting to their walled mansions and gardens, were content with this isolation, and the cutting off all means of communication with the outer world. The people who dwelt in the narrow, pestiferous streets of the city thronged to the churches, and on all sides Heaven was implored to remove its chastening hand from ungodly but repentant Paris.

There was neither willingness nor sufficient intelligence in the people to see a remedy for the evil in the introduction of more air, light and space into the streets of the uncleanly city. They preferred to attribute the infliction to angry saints and an offended God, and the priests did not care to lighten their darkness. When Richelieu ordered the widening of some of the narrow, tortuous lanes, the pulling down of the walls that shut in many of the dirty forecourts, and the space to be thrown into the streets, there were murmurings loud and deep. "It was an interference with the habits of the people," was the general cry. The forecourts of old mean houses sheltered every conceivable nuisance, and there fever, plague and smallpox lurked. Some few of them were at this time done away with, and a freer circulation of air obtained; but the remedy was far too partially applied to effect any sensible improvement in the healthiness of the city.

Notwithstanding the fine hôtels of its nobility and its rich financiers, its Place Royale and fashionable faubourg of the Marais, there were fearful spots in old Paris then, and for many a long year after,—spots where disease was engendered, and where vice and crime were harboured. After dark the rich, besides their usual train of attendants, were accompanied by numerous torch-bearers; but the lives and property of peaceful but less affluent citizens were at the mercy of robbers and assassins, who then left their hiding-places, and with impunity attacked benighted wayfarers in the dreary, unlighted streets; for of police there was actually none, though some ineffectual attempts had from time to time been made towards organizing a watch.

The court had retired to St. Germain; it was

Louis XIII.'s favourite residence, and it was at a convenient distance from Paris. At Versailles there existed then but a poor, dilapidated château, fast falling to ruin, the king, from parsimony, refusing to have it repaired. He was fond of Fontainebleau, but preferred St. Germain because of the greater freedom he enjoyed there; the number of his attendants was fewer, and the courtiers and gentlemen of his household could only be partly lodged in the château of Henry IV. It was rather a hunting-seat than a royal residence affording accommodation for a numerous suite. From prints of the period, it appears to have been elegant in design, though of small extent. It stood on the borders of the then vast forest, where roamed the wild boar and the stag, and which abounded in all sorts of game, strictly preserved for the royal hunt. He was accompanied to St. Germain only by his favourites and companions of the chase; those who could tell the best hunting stories, make him laugh heartily and forget for a time his most dreaded foe — his Satanic majesty.

Louis not only killed his game, but often prepared it for the table. He could lard a piece of meat with the most skilful of his cooks, and was often led to do so, and to display his general knowledge of the culinary art, from his excessive fear of being poisoned, which he further provided against by having every dish set before him tasted by the most trusted of his favourites before he himself partook of it. He possessed talents, however, of a very different order; for he could mount from the kitchen to the painting-room, and produce, as at St. Germain he frequently did, some very pretty and ably-drawn sketches of the surrounding scenery. He also played the théorbe with a masterly hand, and composed many pleasing simple airs for it.

The sound of the guitar, or little mandoline, often drew Louis to the queen's apartment, where Anne of Austria sat curling, combing and frizzing her hair for hours together, while her attendants and ladies praised its beauty. Her small white hands were the constant theme of their admiration; no less so her rounded arm, her pretty foot, her noble figure, and every feature of her face. How often does the diligent Madame de Motteville express her weariness of the frivolous talk and idleness in which so many hours and days were wasted by this "*plus grande reine du monde*"—so she habitually calls her royal mistress, apparently without any satirical intention. Anne would scarcely have cared to undergo the exertion of playing the guitar herself; but she liked to hear it accompanying snatches of Moorish ballads and merry Gitana songs. It reminded her of the Spain she loved, it varied the morning's amusements, and came in as a relief when there was any lull in the "*conversation Espag-*

nole," which consisted in "*des riens galants et mystérieux.*"

When Louis entered, sad, severe, and often suffering in health, the mysterious conversation ceased, but the guitar twanged on, and the singer exerted herself to do her best. If she was the object of his "*chaste galanterie*," he came to gaze upon her. Then, his countenance was watched, and its changing emotions with the changing mood of the Spanish ditty, now tender, grave, or gay. Sometimes his eyes rested on Anne; he did not esteem her, but perhaps he admired her. She possessed her full share of the *embonpoint*, without which it was the fashion of the day to consider no perfection of feature or figure entitled to rank as beauty; and her thirty summers sat lightly and gracefully upon her. Her appearance was that of a woman of twenty-five at the utmost, and but for the fulness of her figure, she would have looked even younger. Louis, on the contrary, might have been credited with forty winters instead of thirty summers. But Anne was not then troubled by cares of state.

Petty political intrigues and private flirtations were her most exciting amusements; and when she got into trouble, she had friends about her sufficiently devoted to risk much to bring her safely out of it; and greatly obliged she was to them at the time, though services rendered to her were apt soon to slip out of her memory. If she had never secured her husband's affections, he had never possessed hers. When accused of conspiring with Gaston for the purpose of afterwards annulling her marriage with Louis and marrying the younger brother, she said it would "not have been worth her while, as she saw no advantage in the change." But though no affection existed between this royal pair, there were also none of the storms and tempests that troubled the peace of Marie de Médicis and Henry IV. Anne contrived, too, to have as much pleasure as her indolent nature needed, and gloomy as the court has been described to be under the influence of the monarch's reserved and inflexible temperament and the severe view he took of his duties, yet it had its under-current of romance, and gaiety was not wholly banished from it. Though the *carrousels* and noisy revels that Marie de Médicis delighted in were suppressed, the court often danced; sometimes from morning till night, and through the night until morning dawned again. Such was the rage for dancing, that even the dismal Louis occasionally figured in a *ballet du roi*.

Great extravagance and eccentricity in dress were also then indulged in, and to such an excess that a court *réunion* resembled a theatrical representation, in which the actors had striven to outdo each other in sumptuousness and variety of toilettes. Not only were immense sums expended on gold embroideries, diamonds, rubies, pearls, point lace, etc., but gentlemen as well as ladies were ambitious of inventing new and eccentric fashions, or introducing modifications of established ones; yet in this attempt the younger part of the fashionable world met with the decided disapproval and opposition of their elders.

The cardinal minister's ostentatious style of living, his military escort, the pomp and parade of royalty he affected — and with the display of which he insulted the oppressed, tax-ridden people, from the fruits of whose labour he exacted his wealth — were little calculated to set an example of moderation to the *haute noblesse*. It rather incited them to attempt to vie with him in the splendour of their elaborately-painted and gold-bedizened, but lumbering equipages, and in the number of their lackeys and attendants; in richness of apparel; in the magnificence of their houses, and the brilliancy of their frequent entertainments.

The king was extremely mean and parsimonious, yet he looked with a jealous eye on all this state and magnificence, so far surpassing his own. The crown jewels were then of small value compared with those possessed by many of the nobility, and though Anne of Austria had most magnificent diamonds and pearls of large size, she brought them from Spain on her marriage. Marie de Médicis had very few jewels.

It was probably for the purpose of pouring a little balm on the sorely-wounded feelings of the king, and of diverting attention from his own assumption of royal state, as well as of pursuing his system of humiliating and crushing the *noblesse*, that Richelieu proposed to prescribe a distinguishing costume for each grade of society. He had the boldness to begin with the *grands seigneurs*, who henceforth were to abate something of that magnificence in dress which it had become their pride to display at court. Red and white plumes, and diamond-looped hats, were not to be laid aside; velvets and satins, and massive embroideries mixed with seed-pearls and gems, fine Venetian lace ruffs, diamond-hilted swords, all might be worn, but varying in degrees of richness with the differing degrees of nobility of the wearers. The class *bourgeoise* and *parlementaire*, the people in their several gradations, all had their costumes assigned them, with some distinctive mark of their calling, or indication of their exact place in the social scale.

Considering the general tendency to turbulence in the nobles of that day, there may have been wisdom in the attempt to mark visibly the separation of classes. For it was inimical to the true interests of commerce and the material prosperity of the nation (which Richelieu, whether for his own glory or not, desired to promote), that the artisans and lower *bourgeoisie* should be drawn away from their occupations and be lured into taking part in the commotions and revolts incited by the disaffected *noblesse*. A sort of order was evoked out of disorder when this classification of the nation was effected and each class ticketed; the inferior classes being made to comprehend that it was to the advantage of each to confine itself to the pursuits or business of its own peculiar sphere. It was a system of separate interests, class against class, that had evil results hereafter. It served at the time to deprive the *noblesse* of a certain degree of influence; to mortify them exceedingly, and equally so to gratify the powerful minister, who struck a further blow at their independence by ordering the demolition of those moated and embattled feudal *châteaux* in the provinces, that were not needed for the defence of the frontiers of the kingdom, or for the protection of the towns. These towns were then mere hamlets or small villages, Paris being sometimes spoken of as "the carbuncle and diamond of the towns of France."

Louis XIII. had a deep sense of his right divine to govern France with an iron sceptre. Considering himself as the incarnation of absolute power derived from God, he could brook no opposition to his will, no observation that seemed contrary to it, except from the cardinal, who sometimes availed himself of his priestly character to read his royal master a lesson. In matters of state he dictated, while affecting to be counselled or consulted; and Louis felt his bondage very sorely at times, but had not the mental power to free himself from the cardinal's strong grasp. His arbitrary measures, however, pleased the king, and the knowledge that his delegated authority was as despotically and unflinchingly used as if directly exercised by himself, to a certain extent consoled him.

But while the court was amusing itself at St. Germain, the plague was raging in Paris. Hundreds died daily, many from fear, many from neglect; but all were carted off to pits at a distance from the city. Gradually the terrible disease subsided. Of those who had fled, some took courage and returned. In most cases their relatives were dead and their houses pillaged; for at no time was robbery more frequent, or crime more prevalent, than during the plague, and while Paris was a scene of general lamentation and woe.

The Hôtel de Rambouillet was not spared. The second son of the marquis, a child of eight years, was stricken by the plague. The marquise was urged to leave the Hôtel, but in vain — she could not be prevailed on to forsake her child. She was reminded that she imperilled her own life, yet she remained firm in her resolve to watch over her son's, and equally firm was Julie d'Angennes in her determination to remain with her mother. The younger daughters and the whole staff of servants were sent into the country. The marquise and her eldest child attended the sufferer ; but notwithstanding their affectionate care, the poor boy died.

For this act of duty, Madame de Rambouillet and Julie were exalted at once into heroines, and, in accordance with the superstitious tendencies of the age, many of their friends saw in the fact of their not having taken the disease, a miracle worked by Heaven in their favour.

CHAPTER XII.

The Duc de Montausier's First Visit to Rambouillet. — Love at First Sight. — A Constant Lover. — Vincent Voiture. —His Sonnets and Letters. — His Letter to Madame de Sainctot. — Voiture *Réengendré*. — De Chavigny's Impromptu. — Voiture's Presumption. — Voiture in Love. — A Wager. — Two Sentinels. — A Privileged Buffoon.

WHEN the plague had passed away from the city, and the period of mourning at Rambouillet was ended, the marquise re-opened her *salons* to her friends. Amongst the many additions to her circle, the most distinguished was the Marquis de Salles — afterwards the celebrated Duc de Montausier. His first visit to Rambouillet forms an epoch in the annals of the famous Hôtel.

The marquis was then just twenty-one. He had heard of the maternal devotion of the marquise and the filial affection of her daughter, and admiration of their conduct induced an anxious desire to know them. The renewal of the receptions of the *salon bleu* afforded him the opportunity of an introduction, which resulted in his falling deeply in love, at first sight, with the charming Julie d'Angennes. Not merely in the sense of becoming her humble servant, according to the laws of chivalry, to be, as then insisted upon, observed by each lady's "*galant et honnête homme*," or, if you please, *cavalier d'amour*. Nothing of the kind. A shaft had gone straight from Cupid's bow deep down into the heart of the young marquis. He was an ardent lover, and fair Julie was disposed to smile graciously upon him. Here, then, the course of true love, one would suppose, might have run on smoothly enough; for the lover was an excellent *parti* (generally the first consideration) and a man of high moral worth. But he had the misfortune, in the eyes of *la belle* Julie's family, to be a Huguenot; consequently his proposal to marry the fair daughter of the House of Rambouillet-Pisani could not be entertained.

The character of the Duc de Montausier has been variously represented: so, indeed, has that of every person of note in the seventeenth century. Some of the numerous memoir and letter writers of the period speak of him as "*le vertueux duc*." Others describe him as captious and disagreeable; *brusque* in manner, and often rude and offensive under an affectation of extreme frankness. A modern writer[*] says, "*Le duc de Montausier est le plus beau caractère qui ait jamais étonné une cour corrompue. Il était l'ennemi du faux en toutes choses.*" And it seems certain that

---

[*] Roederer: "Mémoires pour servir," etc.

he was a man of very high character, incapable of those meannesses and flatteries which characterized the courtiers of his day, and the servile herd that so abjectly worshipped Louis XIV.

The name of the Duc de Montausier is inseparable from that of the Hôtel de Rambouillet and its society, from the date of his first visit there to the death of the marquise. His twelve years of unfailing constancy to Mademoiselle d'Angennes should win for this "Misanthrope" (it is the character of the duke that Molière is supposed to have portrayed in his play of that name) the suffrages of the *beau sexe*. And that gallantry was not incompatible with the severity with which he has been charged, the famous "Guirlande de Julie" sufficiently attests.* Amongst other celebrities who at this time began to frequent the *salon bleu*, were Saint Èvremond, the Abbé Ménage, the sonneteer Benserade, Sarrazin, the eloquent *avocat* Patru, and Scarron, then a gay youth of twenty-one; also the Comtesse de la Suze, la Marquise de Sablé, and other ladies whose *esprit* or poetic talent gave them celebrity in their day.

Vincent Voiture had then returned to Paris, and for none was a warmer welcome awaiting at Rambouillet than for this famous *bel esprit*. Voiture, according to Voltaire, was the first in France to whom the appellation of *bel esprit* was given; beyond which he had but little claim to

* See Chap. XVIII.

renown. It is singular that while Richelieu was striving to separate classes, the Marquise de Rambouillet was endeavouring to assimilate them, and to make intellect and merit rather than feathers and jewels the distinguishing marks of pre-eminence in the society of her Hôtel; to found, in fact, on a community of sentiments, tendencies, and objects, a sort of equality in the social relations.

Voiture, who was so thoroughly at home at Rambouillet that he usually ate and frequently slept there, was the son of a rich vintner of Amiens, who followed the court as its purveyor of wine. He wrote endless pretty sonnets and innumerable letters, none of which he intended for publication beyond that wide circle of friends and acquaintances to whom, by turns, they were addressed. But his letters, like those of Madame de Sévigné, were handed from one to another, read and re-read, copied and re-copied, and distributed far and wide; thus obtaining in the lifetime of the writer a circulation and celebrity more extensive than, probably, in the present day is accorded by the aid of much advertising to many printed works. The pathway to the Temple of Fame would seem to have been an easy one in Voiture's time, to judge from the one printed letter that obtained him an immediate introduction to it, while so many have entered only after long years of toil. It might have been suggested and probably was, for innumerable puns were made on his name, that a *Voiture* would be likely to reach the desired goal with more celerity than a plodder-on, step by step, up the rugged road.

The letter in question, which achieved celebrity for Vincent Voiture, was an ordinary love-letter, addressed to a Madame de Sainctot, with whom he fancied himself in love, but who was far more decidedly in love with him. No promise of talent, no indication of genius appears in it. The style is high-flown and inflated, forced and fantastic in the extreme, yet not witty. But Voiture must have considered it a *chef-d'œuvre* of its kind, as he sent a copy to the Comte d'Avaux (the same who afterwards was one of the plenipotentiaries who signed the Peace of Münster), in a book he had borrowed of him,— Du Rosset's translation of "Ariosto." Voiture, who was fairly educated, had made the acquaintance of the count at the College de Boncourt. Whether as a jest, or from admiration of his fellow-student's production, is not recorded, the count had the letter printed. It was offered for sale, and its success was so astonishingly great, that many thousands of copies were sold. The letter was in everybody's hands, and Voiture's name in everybody's mouth. How Madame de Sainctot liked this publication of her *billet-doux* we are not informed. But probably the name of the lady to whom this famous epistle was addressed was not then made known.

Some friend sent a copy of it to M. de Chaudebonne — *chevalier d'honneur* of the Duchesse d'Orléans — who was very greatly amused by it. Meeting Voiture casually in Paris, he shook him heartily by the hand, and said (as M. Roux, Voiture's biographer, remarks), after the coarse manner of the time, "*Monsieur, vous êtes trop galant homme pour rester dans la bourgeoisie, il faut que je vous en tire.*" M. de Chaudebonne was an intimate friend of Madame de Rambouillet, and it was by an introduction to her that he proposed to raise his *protégé* in the social scale. And Voiture seems in those early days of his fame to have made himself very agreeable to the learned circle generally, and to have amused the ladies especially. After a short probation he was formally received by the marquise, as forming one of the society of the Hôtel. Voiture called his reception within that charmed circle, being "*réengendré par M. de Chaudebonne et Madame de Rambouillet.*"

After this rise in the world, his first patron, the Comte d'Avaux, presented Voiture at court; and M. de Chaudebonne, bringing his interest to bear on the count's, they procured for him the post of "*Introducteur des Ambassadeurs chez Monsieur*," who had taken the title of Duc d'Orléans from the time of his marriage with the rich heiress of Montpensier. This sudden and great advancement Voiture rather presumed upon. His familiarities were often repelled with much indignation, and this "*bourgeois gentilhomme*" received some very severe rebuffs while learning the manners of his new social position. But at the best he was only tolerated, and he appears to have been as much of a buffoon as a wit. Monsieur le Prince said of him one evening at Rambouillet, "*Si Voiture était des nôtres on ne pourrait le souffrir.*" Voiture having been informed of this by a candid friend, replied: "'*Des nôtres*'!

> "Mais c'est bien peu de chose son rang,
> Il n'est que premier prince du sang."

Often he was mortified by direct allusions to his father's business, which his own abstemiousness afforded opportunity for. De Chavigny, afterwards one of the witty and satirical song-writers of the Fronde, remarking one day when dining with Voiture and two other of his friends that he drank but little wine, broke forth with the following offensive impromptu:

> "Quoi! Voiture, tu dégénère!
> Sors d'ici, maugrébier de toy!
> Tu ne vaudras jamais ton père,
> Tu ne vends du vin, ni n'en boy."

But Voiture was not very sensitive, especially in the early part of his career. So long as he was welcomed at the Hôtel de Rambouillet, he was perfectly happy. The young Count de Pisani, the eldest son of the Marquise de Rambouillet, had a very great liking for him, and highly enjoyed his piquant sayings, his witty *impromptus* (known to have been the result of long and careful study), and his frequent practical jokes. On the other hand, the Duc de Montausier felt an extreme aversion towards him, and could see nothing either witty or amusing in his familiar sayings and doings. The duke had a great regard for Mademoiselle de Scudéry, and was in the habit of turning to her when any of Voiture's sallies made the grave literary circle unusually mirthful, with the inquiry: "*Y trouvez-vous de l'esprit? Moi je n'y trouve que de l'impertinence.*"

Voiture, in the excess of his delight at finding himself again in Paris (he had just returned from Lorraine with the Duc d'Orléans), and once more beneath the roof of his loved Hôtel de Rambouillet, was guilty of an unpardonable offence in the eyes of the Duc de Montausier. It also excited the indignation of Julie; and his own apologies and the intercession of his friend Pisani scarcely prevailed on the marquise to pardon it. He had stooped and kissed the arm of Mademoiselle d'Angennes, when permitted, as a great honour on his return, to conduct her from the music-room to the *salon bleu.* Poor Voiture! it was no easy task to make "*un galant et honnête homme*" of him after the pattern of Rambouillet, notwithstanding that his regeneration was accomplished there. Yet he no doubt enlivened the society. Tallemant des Réaux says, "he kept up a perpetual *tintamarre* when at the Hôtel," and that he was really amusing when not in love.

He was apt to fall in love, it appears, and was then extremely stupid, insisting on telling every one the story of his woes; for it was usually one of sadness and sorrow and unrequited love. "Voiture," says Tallemant, "held the erroneous, but amusing opinion, that all knowledge came to a man of good sense and intelligence without any previous study, consequently he himself studied nothing except his numerous *impromptus*." Voiture and young Pisani often amused themselves by guessing who and what the people were who occasionally passed the Hôtel. A grave-looking personage in a coach was guessed one day by Voiture to be "*un homme de la robe*." Pisani made a bet that he was not, Voiture that he was. He undertook also to put the question to the traveller as the only means of deciding the wager. As, with many bows, he advanced towards him, the coach was ordered to stop. Voiture then inquired of its occupant, with apologies, of course, what was his occupation or condition in life. The inquiry was answered only by surprise and indignation. Voiture then explained that it was a wager, and a large sum depending upon it. The supposed "*homme de la robe*," however, declined to afford the requested information, but said he would give the gentleman a piece of advice: "*Gagez*," he said, "*gagez toujours, Monsieur, que vous êtes un sot, et vous ne perdrez jamais.*"

Voiture once met two men near the Rue St. Thomas leading two bears, when it immediately occurred to him, as a good joke, to introduce them stealthily into the Hôtel de Rambouillet. Having succeeded in doing so, he had the animals set up as two sentinels at the door of the marquise's private *cabinet de lecture*, causing, of course, a great deal of alarm and confusion. He took it into his head, on one occasion, when the Comte de Guiche was on a visit to the Marquis de Rambouillet, to wake him up at two o'clock in the morning, saying he had most important news for him. With some difficulty the sleeper was roused sufficiently to inquire what the news was. "M. le Comte," said Voiture, "some time ago you asked me if I was married. I have decided to tell you the truth — I am married." The count stared at him, thinking he was in a dream. At last, as he threw himself into his bed again, he called out: "*Peste! Au diable Voiture, vous et votre femme.*" Voiture seems to have been allowed the privileges of a court fool at the Hôtel de Rambouillet. Yet lucrative places, and sinecures that he sought not, were heaped upon him, and later on, honours that he cared not for — having no inclination to meddle either in politics or diplomacy, though it was his fate to be mixed up in both. All he desired was to make love to Angélique Paulet, and to write fantastic and sentimental letters to her and to the rest of the *belles dames* of Rambouillet.

CHAPTER XIII.

Conrart's Petite Académie. — The Cardinal's Secretary. — Admitted to the Salon Conrart. — Received as Tenth Member. — French Academy founded. — "Le Cid" of Corneille. — The Academy invited to decry it. — "Le Cid" first read in the Salon Bleu. — Le Dictionnaire de l'Académie. — Un Bureau d'Esprit. — The Vicomte de Combalet. — The Widowed Madame de Combalet. — Becomes la Duchesse d'Aiguillon. — The rival Salons. — The Salon Bleu still bears the Palm.

IT had been for some time the custom of a few literary men — nine in number — to assemble on certain evenings at the Hôtel of the rich financier, Conrart, a great patron of literature and himself a writer. Their object was free discussion on learned subjects; also the improvement of the French language, by bringing into discredit certain words in general use by coarse writers of that day, and banishing from familiar conversation those pompous terms in which it was becoming customary to clothe the most simple ideas. These *literati* were all frequenters of the Hôtel de Rambouillet, but at Conrart's private *réunions* — to which they gave the name of the "*Petite Académie*" — they were under far less restraint.

No ladies were present towards whom it was their privilege or irksome duty to play the part of "*galants hommes*," and the etiquette observed in the *salon bleu*—to their great relief, no doubt—was not insisted upon in the Salon Conrart.

The meetings of this select and learned "Council of Nine" soon came to the knowledge of the indefatigable Boisrobert, who was ever ready to play the part of jackal to the lion De Richelieu. Always was he keenly on the watch to snatch at any and every thing that promised to afford but a shred towards the weaving of that cloak of false glory with which the cardinal-minister was to dazzle the eyes of posterity, despite the personal vices it concealed, and the merciless tyranny by which he extinguished the liberties of the people. Boisrobert, therefore, sought admission to the *réunions* of the Salon Conrart. But it was contrary to the rules of the *Petite Académie* to admit outsiders, and as a man of letters, Boisrobert could claim no consideration whatever. He was in repute, in fact, only with his master, and even he valued him less for his small poetic talent than for a certain genial humour and flow of spirits that often dispelled the fits of spleen he was subject to.*

---

* Citois, the cardinal's physician, when summoned to prescribe for his Eminence in his hours of gloom and depression, was accustomed, we are told, after writing his prescription, to add: "No recipe so effectual as a drachm of Boisrobert." And Boisrobert, though a very unclerical personage, was rewarded with the Abbacy of Chatillon-sur-Seine.

Antoine Godeau, who had put the *Bénédicité* into verse, for which the cardinal, for the sake of making a *jeu de mots*, gave him the bishopric of Grasse, was one of the Nine. To him, as having a sort of claim upon his good offices, Boisrobert addressed himself. And, through Godeau's influence, the stringent rule "that no strangers be admitted" was relaxed in favour of the powerful minister's secretary. After reporting to his master what he had done and had seen and heard, he suggested that with a larger number of members and a legal form given to it, such an assembly might become an influential one in the literary world. The suggestion was favourably received by his Eminence. He saw in it both present and future renown, as the patron and protector of men of learning and as the enlightened minister who first, in France, gave an impulse to the cultivation of letters. Boisrobert was authorized to propose, in the cardinal's name, that the *Petite Académie* should extend its limited circle and increase its sphere of usefulness by placing itself under legal sanction.

The proposal was not well received. The little society did not desire the interference of the cardinal. Its members, therefore, deputed Boisrobert to represent to him that by increasing their number and fettering themselves with legal forms, one of the chief objects of their meetings — the spending the evenings together as intimate private friends, in order to discuss freely and irresponsibly certain literary questions, and other topics of interest to them and their host — would at once be at an end. For a time, there the matter rested; but neither Boisrobert nor the cardinal had given it up. The former, by perseverance, obtained admission to the *Petite Académie* as its tenth member. By degrees, and through his influence, eight others were introduced, when the question of "legal form" was again brought on the *tapis* and put to the vote. The original nine voted against it, also one of the new members, so that the cardinal was yet in a minority. Boisrobert still persevered, intrigued and insisted, until the number of members was increased to twenty-eight.

His Eminence himself now appeared on the scene, secure of victory, for his indefatigable secretary had already secured it for him. A majority of the society decided in favour of the cardinal's proposal to found an *Académie Française*, and consequently in 1634 the regulations for the formation of the society were drawn up,— Balzac, Vaugelas, Chapelain and Voiture becoming members. In January, 1635, the letters patent for the legal establishment of the Academy and its forty arm-chairs were given. Those were not the first royal letters authorizing the establishment of an Academy. Charles IX. granted them in 1570 to the poet Antoine de Baïf, and the musician Thibault de Courville, for similar objects, "the improvement and progress of the French language," but the civil war and religious persecutions probably prevented their being acted upon.

To acquire the art of speaking easily and well, with fluency, correctness, and polished diction, was a chief aim of those long conversations at Rambouillet on literary and other given subjects. But the very undue reputation accorded to Voiture had induced a desire to imitate him; consequently, his faults were exaggerated, being easiest of imitation, while his originality, his sole claim to merit, was altogether wanting; and thus both in epistolary writings and in conversation an affected phraseology was introduced under the name of refinement. Voiture was credited with a style both poetic and perfect; but it is laboured in the extreme. It gives one the idea of a striving and writhing after wit; of an effort, not always successful, to produce an epigram in every sentence. Ingenious turns of thought are frequent in his epistles, but one naturally expressed is rarely met with.

The writer of vapid missives to fine ladies was little qualified to sit in judgment on a *chef-d'œuvre* of the grand Corneille, who created the *style tragique*, ennobled the French language, and elevated the genius of the nation. But it was Voiture's fate to be thrust into positions for which he had neither qualification nor inclination, and thus it fell to his lot to be included in that assembly of academicians invited by the cardinal to condemn "Le Cid." It was the first considerable work they had been required to exercise their critical powers upon. Its triumph displeased his Eminence because it was the triumph of genius, and his Academy was expected to decry it; to pronounce it as failing to satisfy in its construction, as a play, the requirements of dramatic art, while as a poem it was poor in thought and sentiment, and wanting in that elevation of style which the loftiness of the subject demanded. But probably neither the cardinal nor the Academy was capable of appreciating Corneille. Duly to estimate his beauties, and to point out his faults, some good models of French dramatic writing on which to form correct judgment and good taste must already have come under the notice of his critics. But none existed. Pierre Corneille was himself the first to offer such a model, and as a pioneer in literature to open the pathway to that excellence attained by the later poets, as also to the acquirement of that harmony, lucidity, and beauty of style, characteristic of the best French prose writers.

All the earlier and best pieces of Corneille were first read in the famous *salon bleu*, and received there the warmest tribute of admiration from its distinguished society. Whether the refinements of Rambouillet were at all influ-

Corneille

P. CORNEILLE

ential in forming the style of Corneille can, of course, only be conjectured; but it may be affirmed that no writings of that period contributed more largely than his towards accomplishing the purely literary objects of the *réunions* of the celebrated marquise. His academical critics had doubtless been present at the first reading of the "Cid," and, like the rest of the company, had approved it. Called upon to condemn, and to award the palm of excellence in dramatic writing to Georges de Scudéry, they refrained from doing so. Their opinions were, however, given with considerable reserve, and some defects, as they conceived, in the conduct of the action of the piece were pointed out, probably that they might not be altogether opposed in their judgment to the wishes of his Eminence.

The French language at the time of the foundation of the Academy retained, like the manners of the age, too many traces of the coarseness and barbarism of the preceding century. As a means towards effecting its desired purification, Chapelain, who, though an inferior poet, was a man of considerable erudition and well acquainted with several languages, suggested to his colleagues the compilation of a standard French dictionary, from which all words whose use was not sanctioned by the Academy should be expunged, and others that it might be desirable to substitute for them introduced. His suggestion was approved of. The famous "*Dictionnaire de l'Académie Française*" was begun, and Chapelain lived to see the work ended, though it was not completed and issued until forty years after. One cause of the delay — the chief one, in fact — was the immense correspondence the undertaking led to, and the number of discussions it occasioned on the rejection, adoption and retention of a variety of words.

The head-quarters of *la société polie* had, naturally, a voice in the matter. Julie d'Angennes, in a series of letters in a lively strain, contended successfully with the learned academicians for the retention of the useful word *car*, which they had proposed to abolish. It was then in too frequent use, and a stiff and laboured style of writing was the result. By its means "*des gentillesses*," to quote the words of M. Taine, "*s'allongeaient en phrases aussi concertées qu'une dissertation académique.*" Still it was not desirable to suppress it altogether; and probably the Academy could not have done so, especially as no acceptable equivalent was offered for it. But it was well to call attention to and to deprecate its unsparing use, so common in the writings of that day.

A rival *salon* now offered its attractions to the academicians and *gens de lettres* generally.

Most appropriately it was that of the niece of their patron, who was about to exchange his red hat for a helmet, and to assume the spear and shield. A herald, armed *cap-à-pie*, had been sent to Brussels to declare in the name of the potent Louis XIII. his hostile intentions against his brother-in-law and cousin of Spain, and the cardinal and the king were going to the wars.* The former determined that France should be a terror to her enemies and neighbours, however wretched and depressed her people might be under his grinding despotism at home. In his absence his band of poets would be welcomed by his niece, who aspired to a literary reputation, and whose lover he was. Her *salon* at the Petit Luxembourg — where she lived in a style corresponding to the magnificence so ostentatiously displayed by her uncle — had already obtained the name of the "*bureau d'esprit.*"

In 1620, when Richelieu — or rather Du Plessis, for he was then only Bishop of Luçon — was residing in seclusion at Avignon, and sharing to some extent in the disgrace that Marie de Médicis had brought on herself by countenancing the misrule of her favourite Concini, he married this niece, then a girl of fifteen, to the Vicomte Antoine de Combalet. She appears to have disliked him extremely; but feeling, as we know, was

* This was the last occasion, 1635, on which a herald was sent to announce a declaration of war.

not then taken into account in such matters, when otherwise the match was desirable. So great was her aversion to him, that she fell into a melancholy and desponding state that affected both her mind and her health.

Recalled to court two years after and raised to the dignity of cardinal, through the interest of Marie de Médicis, Richelieu obtained for M. de Combalet the command of a detachment of troops destined to harass the Huguenots. In this expedition he was killed, as it was expected he would be, or — if he failed to answer the expectations of his friends — intended that he should be. His widow immediately retired to the convent of the Carmelites; by no means with a desire to take the veil, but to remain *en retraite* for the first year of her widowhood. On the expiration of that year, alarmed lest she should again be forced into a marriage opposed to her inclinations, she took vows of seclusion for twelve months, and twice renewed them. But as her uncle grew wealthy and powerful, his ambition led him to aspire to a very brilliant *parti* for the young widow -- even (as Tallemant des Réaux asserts) Gascon d'Orléans, the king's brother.

Whether true or not that such was Richelieu's vain ambition, Madame de Combalet neither married Gascon nor any second husband. No longer a timid girl, she left the Carmelites and entered the gay society of the world of fashion; by degrees casting aside every vestige of widow's dress, and, contrary to long-established custom, wearing colours. This innovation found favour with the widowed part of the *beau monde*, and Madame de Combalet's example was very generally followed. To her it is owing that French widows may, if they so choose, wear any colour but green,—green did not suit her complexion, therefore, for widows' use, a strict embargo was laid upon it. By-and-by the kind uncle installed his niece in the Petit Luxembourg, which he furnished with extraordinary splendour; and as even the name of De Combalet was particularly distasteful to her, in 1632 he bought the lands that constituted the domain of the Duchy of Aiguillon and presented them to her. The estate carried with it the title, and henceforth Madame de Combalet was known only as la Duchesse d'Aiguillon.

The *salon* of the Petit Luxembourg never acquired either the vogue or literary celebrity of that of the Hôtel de Rambouillet. It was darkened by the shadow of Richelieu, who was hated even more than he was feared. The duchess was also greatly under the influence of le Père Vincent de Paul, of whose zeal in establishing religious houses and founding asylums and refuges the Parliament openly complained, saying it threatened to fill Paris with idle vagrants and illegitimate children. The court, the literary world, and the Church, each by turns, was, therefore, in the ascendant. Sometimes the political intrigues of the cardinal, at others the awakened conscience and consequent *retraite* of the hostess, suspended the *séances littéraires;* while the various conflicting public and private interests that agitated the society of the period, but which lay dormant in the neutral atmosphere of Rambouillet, formed naturally a disturbing element, though the expression of it was suppressed in the company frequenting the *salon* of the great minister's niece.

There was no easy unrestrained flow of conversation; for who could be sure that a spy did not lurk under the pleasant exterior of some apparently genial guest of the duchess? or that some harmless or thoughtless expression might not be tortured into a sign of the disaffection of the speaker towards the powers that ruled? Possibly, too — one fears to say probably, for even at Rambouillet, though the manners were punctilious, it was not because the society was really very strait-laced — possibly, then, some one, two, or even three *grandes dames* of that day might not have chosen to give their countenance to the cardinal's niece, and to a *liaison* which was so repugnant to the severe principles of Louis XIII., that on account of it and other irregularities of the cardinal's private life, he for a considerable time refrained from raising him to the post of minister. That he eventually did so was because the weak mind fell under the dominion of the strong one, and henceforth the king merely reigned while the cardinal governed. But Louis had, at least, the consolation of knowing that no man was so well qualified as Richelieu to carry out his despotic views and his notions of the absolute authority with which he believed kings were divinely invested.

But to return to the Petit Luxembourg: it was not a success; and in spite of the finely painted ceilings, for which it was celebrated, and the almost regal decorations of the *salons*, the more simple but tasteful and elegant *salon bleu* still bore away the palm, and experienced no falling off in the number of its literary and other distinguished guests. Yet the cardinal's stringent measures to secure the separation of classes did not extend to the receptions of his niece, and exclusiveness was no more the rule in the "*bureau d'esprit*" of the duchess than in the *salon littéraire* of the marquise. But the latter may have been the more pleasing hostess; her family group, too, was attractive: *la belle* Julie, staid and statuesque; her younger sister, lively and coquettish; the youthful Count Pisani, the heir of the House of Rambouillet, and its good-humoured genial head, the marquis. He, indeed, was frequently employed in diplomatic affairs, but when at home was proud to be the "*galant homme*" of his marquise, whom he regarded in all respects as "the first of womankind."

CHAPTER XIV.

Contrasts and Changes in French Society. — The World and the Cloister. — Vincent a Popular Confessor. — He retires to the Oratoire. — Preceptor to the Sons of De Gondy. — Spiritual Director of Louis XIII. — Successful Appeals for Alms. — The Sisters of Charity. — L'Hôpital des Enfants Trouvés. — Le Commandeur de Sillery. — Story of Vincent's Earlier Life. — The Captive Greek. — Vincent a Friend to the Poor.

MANY contrasts, no less striking than strange, are presented by the changes that took place in the manners and habits of French society from the beginning to the close of the seventeenth century. Singularly, too, the career of almost every woman of high rank who acquired celebrity during any part of that century, offers in the various phases of its own often short span an epitome of the changing moods of the outward life of the whole period. First, the ignorance and superstition of early years, resulting from convent training. Next, a plunge into the dissipations of a depraved court and an immoral age — irregularities of conduct being glossed over with a varnish of false sentiment and affected refinements of speech and manner. Then, temporary withdrawal, after a satiety of the so-called pleasures of the world, to the seclusion of some fashionable religious retreat, for the occasional discipline of a horsehair chemise. Or, as then too often happened, to hide forever in the gloom of the cloister a once lovely face, now disfigured by that dreaded bane of beauty, small-pox. Or, again, when the charms of youth had fled, to seek compensation in the deference paid to the airs and graces of assumed piety when faded coquettes became severe devotees.

Just as in the latter part of his reign, and after a dissolute life, the change of fashion in his court from depravity to religion — or rather the hypocritical semblance of it — quieted the qualms of conscience that had begun to disturb the magnificent Louis XIV., who is said to have looked forward to continuing his *rôle* of Grand Monarque even in the next world. And not only the servility of his courtiers was calculated to confirm him in this expectation, if he really entertained it — and it is not unlikely — but even that of the great court-preachers of the day, who made him the hero of their discourses; which for the greater part were but eloquent panegyrics of the God of Versailles, before whom it was almost sacrilege to hint that there existed a greater God than he.

The Duchesse d'Aiguillon was one of those *grandes dames* who long balanced between love of this world and fear of losing the next. After the death of her uncle, she fell entirely under the control of her confessor, Vincent de Paul, who is represented as of gentle and insinuating manners, "*qui plaisaient beaucoup aux pécheresses repentantes.*" He was so mild, so indulgent, that he readily excused all faults; so candid that he willingly acknowledged the weakness of poor human nature and its liability to trip. He first became popular with the ladies of the court as a confessor from having filled that office very satisfactorily to the Princess Marguérite, first wife of Henry IV., during the last two or three years of her life, when, as her biographer says, "*elle était vouée à la piété.*"

But this inclination to excuse, to indulge, to pardon others, was so excessive, that "M. Vincent himself was drawn into some forgetfulness of the severity of the laws of ecclesiastical discipline."* He even thought it necessary to abide for a time with the religious confraternity of les Pères de l'Oratoire. This vast foundation owes its origin in France to le Père Pierre de Berulle, afterwards cardinal. Its establishment was based on the idea that, however pure a man's life may be, he has his moments of weakness, of faint-heartedness and want of moral force, when it would be useful to open to him a house of retreat where he could collect his thoughts, and by meditation, and especially by

* See "Vie de Vincent de Paul," par Capefigue.

prayer, regain strength of mind. Hence the name of l'Oratoire. The establishment was under the direction of le Père de Berulle. He was the friend of Vincent who with him first visited Paris.

To De Berulle he confessed on the occasion of the weakness referred to — which is said to have been allowing love to slip unawares into his susceptible heart — all the errors and moral failures of his life. For two years this really kindly-natured, sympathizing and tender-hearted priest struggled with feelings which might, perhaps, have been more easily overcome by active occupation in the world than by solitude and meditation. He is supposed, however, to have thoroughly subdued them when he left the Oratoire, though, in some sort as a further penance, and to restrain a naturally impetuous imagination, De Berulle induced him to accept the small curacy of Clichy. But he soon resigned it, and became preceptor to the three sons of Emanuel de Gondy, Comte de Joigny — his youngest pupil being the witty, intriguing, turbulent and famous coadjutor of Paris of the time of the Fronde, Jean François de Gondy, afterwards Cardinal de Retz.

The Comte de Joigny, according to an anecdote, said to be authentic, was induced by Vincent to renounce the practice of duelling,— every dispute, every difference of opinion, was then settled by a duel, and no gentleman could refuse to draw his sword when his adversary, who might be his most intimate friend, demanded a meeting. Every duel of consequence — that is, where each party to it considered his honour especially concerned in maintaining himself, however much in the wrong in the quarrel, to be essentially in the right — was preceded by mass and communion; for one, if not both, of the antagonists must look for death. This law of the middle ages was still observed — that "each cavalier when he faced his adversary must be in a state of grace — ready also to face his God."

The Comte de Joigny, preparing himself for a duel of this kind, had just finished his devotions, and was leaving the chapel where Vincent had officiated, when a few solemn words fell on his ear, as if of a voice from Heaven commanding him to stay. Somewhat startled, he turned back a step. He was face to face with his priest, who had followed him, and who at once began earnestly to expatiate on the wickedness and folly of the act he was about to engage in. Vincent had the gift of speaking powerfully and impressively, and in this case seems to have used it most effectively. For the count gave up the duel, and, lowering the point of his sword, swore an oath upon it never again to take part in one, — a proof of the possession of great moral courage, for any gentleman refusing a duel might then be openly branded with cowardice.

After Vincent became the spiritual director and confessor of Louis XIII., he was accustomed to say mass every Friday in the chapel of the Louvre, where the court, as well as all who were distinguished for charity and piety, rarely failed to assemble. When the service was ended, it was the custom of Vincent to address his congregation on behalf of some one of his numerous charities. Having worked on the feelings of his attentive listeners by harrowing descriptions, which were probably not overdrawn, of the misery and wretchedness of the unfortunates for whom he was pleading, and told the sympathizing *grands seigneurs et dames* how a little self-denial might alleviate great suffering, he would suddenly produce from under his surplice the bag or purse for the collection of the alms, and pass it round to them. The ladies vied with each other in their eagerness to fill it with gold and jewels; for in their enthusiasm they divested themselves of all such superfluities to supply the needs of the poor.

No preacher of the day was so successful as Vincent in his appeals for alms. And he was not always solemn or severe; for he was a true Gascon, and could effectively mingle wit and pleasantry in his most earnest addresses. He has been thought to have presented his bag rather too often, and his enemies have also accused him of amassing wealth. But as he left no wealth, and had so many charities to provide for, it is only fair to believe that although he collected large sums and received grants of lands and considerable donations of money, the demands upon his resources were so heavy that little or none was left for hoarding. He established the foundling hospital, the asylum for poor lunatics, that for fallen and repentant women, and several schools for the instruction of poor children of both sexes in Paris and the villages around it.

The non-cloistered community of the sisters of charity was also founded by Vincent de Paul. All the younger ladies were immediately bent on joining it, and becoming nurses at the hospital of the Hôtel Dieu. But after a very short experience of the nature of the duties involved in this new vocation, they readily followed the advice of their director to leave the nursing to more competent hands, and to content themselves with serving the cause of charity by contributing pecuniarily to the support of the institutions. Another sisterhood, "*les sœurs grises*," founded by the wealthy Madame Legros, at the suggestion of Vincent, was occupied wholly in teaching the poor children of his schools.

Frightful disorder reigned at that time amongst the inferior order of the clergy. Vincent was desirous of reforming so deplorable a state of things, and compelling a stricter observance of priestly discipline. In this he met with violent opposition, and his projects for the benefit of the poor were criticized and condemned by those clerical reprobates. He himself rather discouraged the founding of new monasteries and convents, believing there were more opportunities of serving God in the world than in the cloister. An opinion which gained him many enemies in the Church.

Paris was a den of vice and infamy at the time of Vincent de Paul's greatest activity and zealous perseverance in founding charitable institutions. His project for the asylum of "*Les enfants trouvés*" met with some remonstrance and condemnation, as encouraging crime. But the horrid sights he had witnessed in connection with the exposure of poor infants in the holes, and corners, and kennels, and masses of filth, where dogs, and cats, and rats found food, had moved him to pity. They are too revolting in their details to be reproduced here. "*Tristes spectacles!*" says a French writer, "*dûs aux plaisirs du temps.*" But they were due in part also to the frequent visitations of famine and plague; so that in rescuing those wretched children from a miserable death, Vincent de Paul saved also many a wretched mother from a crime which misery and want might have driven her to. Madame Fremiot de Chantal (the grandmother of Madame de Sévigné), who was canonized for her great piety, was one among the many who aided him in establishing this and other charitable foundations.

The Duchesse d'Aiguillon devoted the greater part of her income to the same objects, as well as for sending missionaries to "*les parties sauvages de la France,*" ransoming slaves, and setting prisoners free. The Commandeur de Sillery, who had been French ambassador at Rome, was so much impressed by the exhortations and the example of Vincent, that he sold his fine hôtel, its splendid furniture, rare pictures and treasures of art, in order to aid him in carrying out his various projects for the relief of the suffering poor. He also dismissed his entire household, and after providing for a few small pensions to ancient servitors of his family, and strictly limiting his own expenditure to a sum just sufficient for the necessaries of life, made a gift of the whole of his revenue to the Hôtel Dieu. An excess of charity which none other of the *noblesse* seems to have imitated, though a similar disposal of an immense fortune was made by the young widow of the President Goussault.

There was a tinge of romance in the earlier history of Vincent which gave him an additional interest in the eyes of enthusiastic ladies. And he could tell the story of his adventures as effectively as he could plead the cause of suffering humanity. He was indeed well fitted for his vocation, and for the age in which he lived. While on a voyage to Marseilles on some business for his father, who was a shepherd farmer and the owner of large flocks, he was taken prisoner by a Barbary pirate and sold as a slave. He was first bought by a fisherman, who treated him well as long as he worked hard. Being compelled to part with him, Vincent's next purchaser was an astrologer. This man took a fancy to him, behaved kindly, and perceiving his intelligence (he had but recently left the university of Toulouse to be ordained priest by the Bishop of Tarbes) initiated him in the mysteries of his art. In the course of a year or two the astrologer died. Vincent was again led to the slave-market, and was then bought by a renegade Greek in the service of the Grand Turk.

He now first found opportunity for the exercise of that great moral influence he afterwards so powerfully exerted, over women especially. The Greek had a captive Christian wife to whom he was greatly attached, and at whose entreaty he was inclined to give Vincent his freedom. But before an opportunity for doing so had occurred, they together so worked on his feelings as to induce him to embrace Christianity, and to seek an occasion for escaping with his wife and Vincent to France. This he succeeded in doing, and at Avignon the Greek publicly embraced the Christian faith. This conversion, ascribed to the persuasive teaching of Vincent, gained him great favour at Rome, whither he immediately proceeded. Paul V., the great patron of the arts, was much pleased with him, as were also le Père de Berulle and the Comte de Joigny, in whose family he became preceptor.

The stories, humorous and pathetic, of his captivity, he is said to have often related for the amusement or edification of his patrons and patronesses, and to have told them charmingly, touchingly and persuasively. There was nothing studied in his expressions or his manner; he apparently spoke from real emotion and from his heart. "Goodness, cheerfulness, even gaiety seemed to breathe in and to inspire his every word and every look. It was difficult not to love him." Such, we are told, was Vincent de Paul. And although it is acknowledged that he was "*tant soit peu rusé*, and used adroitly *une douce finesse et une grande habilité*" in obtaining funds for the amelioration of the condition of the then very helpless and little-cared-for poor, sick, aged and infirm; yet it must be admitted that he did much good in his generation, and that his memory deserves to be held in honour far more than that of many who have been promoted by the Church of Rome to the honour of saintship. In the next century his statue bore the inscription — "Au Chrétien Philosophe."

CHAPTER XV.

Début of Mdlle. de Bourbon-Condé. — Her Toilette and her Cilice. — Her Desire to take the Veil. — Her Parents refuse their Consent. — Introduced at Rambouillet. — Armed against Satan's Assaults. — Anne of Austria. — The Cilice admonishes in Vain. — Anne de Bourbon converted. — The New Star and her Adorers. — The Château de Chantilly. — Its Gardens and Grounds. — Amusements of the Guests. — The Letter-Bag. — A Letter from Voiture. — Tossed in a Counterpane. — Marriage of Anne de Bourbon. — " The Cook's Daughter." — The Marquise de Sablé. — Beauty of Madame de Longueville. — An Attack of Small-pox.

HERE was a *grand ballet de la reine* at the Louvre on February 18th, 1635, and the *Gazette de France* names Mademoiselle Anne Géneviève de Bourbon-Condé as one of the sixteen young ladies who danced in it. She was the daughter of Monsieur le Prince, and was born, as before mentioned, in the Château de Vincennes in 1619, during her father's imprisonment there. She was but in her sixteenth year when first introduced, at this ball, to the society of the court. And great was the sensation she occasioned. The cheek of many a bright belle paled with envy, the heart of many a gay cavalier fluttered with the first emotions of love, as the still beautiful Princesse de Condé led in her trembling daughter and presented her to the queen. For one so young and fair her dress was of extraordinary magnificence (a portrait of her thus attired still exists). It was of white brocade, with puckerings of fine lace divided by strings of pearls; the sleeves were looped with large diamonds; the same brilliant gems glittered on her bosom, sparkled like dew-drops in the rays of the morning sun on the leaves of the bouquet she wore, and shone in the masses of golden hair that fell in long curls on her fair shoulders.

Amongst the glistening diamonds dropped a glistening tear when those downcast eyes of heavenly blue were raised to the queen's. Anne of Austria remarked it with surprise, the princess with a glance of displeasure. The queen spoke encouragingly to the timid girl; but neither the queen nor the princess was aware that beneath her splendid *toilette*, Mademoiselle de Bourbon wore a small corset or *cuirasse* or horse-hair bandage, called *un cilice;* a minor form of torture to fret and irritate the skin and prevent her from taking any pleasure at this ball, to which she had been brought entirely against her will. She had received what was called her education at the Carmelite Convent in the Rue St. Jacques. There, naturally very impressionable, her mind had been worked upon by the exhortations of narrow-minded superstitious nuns and much reading of the lives of mythical saints, until Mademoiselle de Bourbon, at the age of fifteen, expressed a wish to take the veil as a Carmelite nun.

Le Père Lejeune, her confessor, encouraged this fancy, for Mademoiselle de Bourbon would carry with her to the cloister a very large fortune. But Monsieur le Prince, who was known for his avarice and love of wealth, was by no means inclined to give his only daughter and her large inheritance to the Church. He refused his consent to any such scheme, and desired that it might never again be even mentioned. She was to marry, and keep up the *prestige* and social influence of the family. The princess was blamed by her husband for not having discovered and sooner checked this foolish whim. She herself was extremely devout,—frequently retiring to the fashionable Carmelite Convent for a few days of meditation and prayer. She and the prince were not often agreed in opinion, but in this instance they were perfectly in harmony. The one lovely daughter who had inherited the beauty of her mother — beauty that had stirred so deeply the pulses of a grey-bearded king — must not waste her sweetness on the desert air of a cloister and fade away in the gloom of a convent.

But it was not so easy a matter to turn the young lady from her purpose. Though removed from the convent, she confided all her sorrows to the nuns on those days when she still was allowed to pass an hour or two with them. Monsieur le Prince was too powerful a personage directly to oppose, but they could comfort and cheer their devout pupil with hopes that, if her firmness remained unshaken, she yet might enter their doors to pass out of them no more. And what were all the *fêtes* and *carrousels*, the balls and shows of the sinful world, compared with the shows of the Church? the magnificent vestments, the pictures, the sculpture, the music, the incense, the gentle sisters, the convent's angelic peace? — peace too often born of despair!

It was determined by her parents that, although so young, she should begin to frequent general society before her *début* at court, and accordingly Mademoiselle de Bourbon was introduced at Rambouillet. But whether that the great interest then taken there in the proposed rejection of many words in the language had so fully engrossed the attention of the company that they could give heed to no other objects, or that the new visitor cared not whether *prouesses* gave place to *grandes actions* or *pensers* to *pensées* — (these words being then under discussion by the dictionary people) — it is certain that no favourable impression was either made or received by this pouting young damsel who was resolved to be a nun. The same want of success attended her introduction at the Hôtel of the Duchesse de Liancourt, who had also begun to receive a select circle of the *beau monde* and *gens de lettres.* The princess, disappointed and grieved, could not refrain from bitterly reproaching her daughter. She is said to have replied: "*Vous avez, Madame, des grâces si touchantes que comme je ne vais qu'avec vous, et ne parais qu'après vous, on ne m'en trouve point.*" An answer worthy of Rambouillet, and which showed that mademoiselle had already some insight into character — for Madame la Princesse could never forget that her beauty had created a sensation, and that she was still considered *belle,* and really was *jeune encore.*

At length the prince himself announced to his daughter that she would be required in three days from that time to appear at a ball to be given by the queen at the Louvre, and that she would have to take her part in the *ballet de la reine.* Poor mademoiselle! To most girls this would have been a delightful piece of news, to her it was a sorrowful one. Entreaties to be excused were of no avail. Any appearance of intention to resist the parental will would be met, she was assured, by the exercise of parental authority to enforce it. Great was the consternation, the affliction, the embarrassment of the Carmelites. They could not advise her to obey — they dared not counsel her to disobey. After long musing a brilliant thought, as if by inspiration, came suddenly into the mind of the abbess. It was to arm the victim against the assaults of Satan with a shield, in the shape of a horse-hair *cuirasse.* The nuns warmly approved, and the vestment was immediately provided and stealthily placed upon her. At the same time they warned her to be constantly on her guard and unfailing in her attention to the admonitory scratchings of the *cilice*. Her faith in it, like theirs, was unbounded; her self-confidence not less. Forth then she went, arrayed in gold and gems that added no charm to her beauty, to prove, as she felt, how powerless were all the vain pleasures of the world to lure her from the path of piety she had chosen.

The plumed, diamond-decked and lace-bedizened courtiers had assembled in full force that evening. The ladies — a glittering throng, frizzed and rouged and fluttering their jewelled Moorish fans — attended as numerously. Hundreds of waxlights illumined the vast *salon*, at the farther end of which, in a large crimson velvet and gold-fringed arm-chair, sat Anne of Austria, Louis's neglected wife. She was splendidly dressed and was a royal-looking woman, though at that time far less beautiful than some writers have described her; for she had grown large and lazy, and was far too highly rouged. But her coquettish *agacerie* and grace in the use of her fan were peculiarly Spanish, and imparted a degree of animation to her rather indolent air. She was always gracious in manner, and on this occasion was listening with smiling satisfaction to the complimentary speeches of the Duc de Beaufort, Henry IV.'s grandson, who was ever assiduous in paying his court to her.

But why, as with downcast eyes she passed through this brilliant throng, did the youthful Anne de Bourbon shed tears? Did she feel her weakness already? or was it that the admonitory *cilice* was tearing and fretting her delicate skin? Not even Victor Cousin, who, in his " Femmes illustres" has so delighted to speculate on the feelings and to expatiate on the beauty of this *belle* of the seventeenth century, has told us more than simply that she shed tears. But her bright eyes, "those eyes of Heaven's deepest blue," were soon dried. "What should she fear?" Her place in the dance is assigned her, a gay cavalier presses her hand as he conducts her to it, and whispers compliments that are new to the ear of this emotional young girl. Her colour is heightened, her eyes sparkle, and her rosy mouth smiles. In vain the *cilice* scratches, she heeds it not, for she is actually enjoying the dance she had so much dreaded. And so the evening passes away. All eyes have been upon the youthful *belle* of the ball, and her cheek has glowed with proud delight in the consciousness of the admiration her beauty excited.

Three in the morning! a horribly dissipated hour to be abroad in old Paris. Yet the two or more loud-sounding clocks of the city had struck three full half an hour before the *calèche* of Madame la Princesse was on its way back to the Hôtel de Condé. Mademoiselle sat between her parents, a hand clasped by each. But she was silent, and a little agitated by emotions hitherto unknown to her; emotions of delight, which the sharp admonitions of the *cilice* proved powerless to subdue. Henceforth, she is a changed person!

Who now so gay and joyous as the lately sad and pining Anne de Bourbon? A kindly feeling towards her mourning Carmelite friends she still retains, but her affections are transferred from the cloister to the world. Her desire is now to shine in that world, and to conquer. To effect so sudden and thorough a conversion, this *ballet de la reine* must have been a very brilliant affair. Contemporary writers, with but few exceptions, speak of them generally as mere scenes of coarse gaiety. Yet as *spectacles* only — from the splendour of the costumes, particularly those of the *grands seigneurs* who vied with each other in the magnificence of their dresses — they must have been very imposing.

Of this particular *ballet*, in which all the beauties of the court are said to have figured, it was observed with more gallantry than reverence, that on leaving the Louvre "*chacun remportait de ce lieu plein de merveilles la même idée que celle de Jacob, lequel n'ayant vu toute la nuit que des anges, crut que c'était le lieu où le ciel joignait avec la terre.*"

The Hôtel de Rambouillet next welcomed the new star, wondering behind what cloud it had concealed itself on its first appearance there. The receptions at the Hôtel de Condé, though the Prince was no general favourite, drew from the famous Rambouillet many of its least literary *habitués*. But whether at their own Hôtel, the Petit Luxembourg, the Palais Cardinal, the Hôtels of the Place Royal, or at the Louvre, a crowd of adorers followed in the train of Mademoiselle Anne de Bourbon. Such continual worship and ceaseless incense of flattery might well have turned an older and wiser head, for she was little more than a child in years,—not yet sixteen, though taller, and in figure more fully developed, than girls of her age usually are.

When the spring was more advanced, the princess and her daughter accompanied the court to Fontainebleau, whence they proceeded to Chantilly, where they assembled a little court of their own. It was as necessary as it was customary then to secure a large party to amuse and be amused at these lovely *châteaux de province* of the *grands seigneurs*. There the ladies regulated life after the manner of Astrée, and the pastorals of Calprenède and Gomberville. For until the deeds of arms of the great Condé (as yet but a boy of fourteen) inspired the pen of Mademoiselle de Scudéry, and "Le Grand Cyrus" appeared, Phyllis and Strephon and their *honnête amitié* lost nothing of their *prestige.* The wide domain of Chantilly had long been the property of the Montmorenci family, when it passed into the possession of the Condés after the execution for treason of the last unfortunate duke; and thus Chantilly, with its *château* dating anterior to the Renaissance, became a standing souvenir of the two great military families of ancient France, — that of the illustrious Anne de Montmorenci, constable of the kingdom, under Francis I., and of Louis de Bourbon, Prince de Condé.*

Chantilly was the favourite residence of Madame la Princess, and it was a charming *séjour* in the fine part of the year. If its gardens were rather staid and formal, as was the style of the period, there was much that was picturesque in the grounds, and the forest in summer and autumn was a scene of wild beauty. Vincent Voiture was greatly in request at several of these princely *châteaux*, so also was Sarrazin, and later on Mathieu Montreuil; agreeable writers of sonnets and of pretty conceits in verse, and possessing some reputation for lively wit. A *bel esprit* must have been a desirable addition to those rather insipid parties of twenty or thirty ladies and gentle-

---

* In Perelle's "Grands Châteaux de France" there are views of the château, grounds, and gardens, as they existed in the latter years of the grand Condé, who took great pride in improving and embellishing them.

men playing at shepherds and shepherdesses. Here and there a fool still formed one of the retainers of an old baronial establishment. But fools had gone out of fashion and favour since Voiture had introduced practical joking and buffoonery as the qualifications of a *bel esprit*.

Those minor poets of the hour wrote the greater part of the amatory verses in which the shepherds were expected to make love to their shepherdesses. For though rhyming was the rage, all had not the faculty of telling in rhymes of the amorous flame that was supposed to be consuming them. The mornings were spent in this literary love-making. In the afternoon, while the ladies trifled over their embroidery-frames, the most ungallant of the gentlemen lounged off by themselves. Those that remained read for the general amusement some part of the long spun-out romances of the day. In the summer evenings the whole party set out together for a promenade in the grounds, but generally returned in straggling couples; it was so easy for those who wished it to wander from the right path in those mazy thickets and woods. When the party reassembled, there were sports, and games, and music (singing with lute accompaniment), in the apartment of Madame la Princesse, and if Monsieur le Prince happened to be at the *château*, there was a good deal of gambling in his.

On the whole there was no lack of employment and pastime, and no doubt life was a pleasant thing at one's *château* in these good old times, far away from the plague and the famine, the dirt and the squalor of Paris. Imagine all those grandees loitering round the fish-ponds and feeding the fishes — what a pretty sight! or assembled on the broad terrace refreshing themselves with champagne (for champagne was then no less esteemed by the ladies than it is now. And more deservedly so, as it was then pure *vin de champagne*, not a fizzing concoction of heaven knows what, prepared for the English market). Or behold them, in fancy, sauntering over that broad sweep of greensward, while others are reading D'Urfé in the balconies, and some three or four of those charming *seigneurs* in velvet and satin are stretched on the grass, their Spanish hats and feathers, and swords lying beside them. One cavalier jumps up, a bright belle takes his arm, and they stroll off together for a confidential conversation through the shady *allées* of the park.

Then the letter-bag arrives, and causes no small commotion; it comes at all hours, often when least expected, but by no means every day. How welcome those news-letters are, not only to the fortunate recipient, but to those who hear them read. They contain the gossip of the *salons* of Paris, the gallantries and the intrigues of the court. There is not much to tell of the doings of the king; but of the insolent airs and the extravagant dress of his present favourite, Cinq Mars, and of the toleration this meets with from the cardinal, many hints, but very guarded hints, are given. There is a letter also from Voiture, it is addressed to Mademoiselle Anne de Bourbon, and as it tells of the tossing in a counterpane at Rambouillet, where one would have supposed nothing so undignified could ever have taken place, it may be as well to let this famous *bel esprit* tell the story himself, observing only that the company at Rambouillet had been amusing themselves by playing at "forfeits." Voiture had been desired to say or do something that, within a certain number of minutes, should make them laugh. He had undertaken to do so, and failed. This failure was deemed a punishable offence, and Madame de Rambouillet, at the request of Julie and Angélique Paulet (who could have believed it?), decreed that poor Voiture should be tossed in a counterpane as many times as he had been allowed minutes to accomplish the feat he had failed in.

He writes:

"Elles en avoient remis l'exécution au retour de Madame la Princesse et de vous. Mais elles s'avisèrent depuis qu'il ne fallait pas remettre des supplices à une saison qui devoit être toute destinée à la joie. J'eus beau crier et me defendre: la couverture fut apportée, et quatre dés plus forts hommes du monde furent choisis pour cela. Ce que je vous puis dire, Mademoiselle, c'est que jamais personne ne fut si haut que moi, et que je ne croyois pas que la fortune me dut jamais tant élever. Je vis les montagnes abaissées au dessous de moi; je vis les vents et les nuées cheminer dessous mes pieds; je decouvris des pays que je n'avais jamais vu et des mers que je n'avoit point imaginées. Mais je vous assure, Mademoiselle, qu'on ne voit tout cela qu'avec inquiétude lorsque l'on est en l'air et que l'on est assuré d'aller retomber."

And thus Voiture continues, for a page or two, to recount what he pretended to have seen in the clouds, as he rose and fell at each toss of the counterpane. He delighted in writing letters filled with absurdities and affectations to the Rambouillet circle; and his admirers considered them ample atonement for the freedoms and liberties he had constantly to be reminded of, and often to submit to some ridiculous punishment for. However, he had his reward in the pensions and sinecures his friends were ever on the alert to secure for him.

But to return to Mademoiselle de Bourbon: when she again appeared in the *"société polie"* of Paris it was as Duchesse de Longueville. On completing her sixteenth year her marriage had almost immediately taken place. The bridegroom was a widower of forty, with a daughter but two years younger than his bride. It was, of course, a mere *mariage de convenance*. But there were advantages in it that outweighed the consideration — no light one with the haughty princess — that Henri, Duc de Longueville, was scarcely of equal rank with the family of Bourbon-Condé. His escutcheon bore a bar sinister; he was a descendant of the famous *"jeune et brave* Dunois," an illegitimate scion of the House of Orléans, and the hero of the well-known French national song, the music of which is attributed to Queen Hortense, the mother of Napoleon III.

La grande Mademoiselle de Montpensier, referring in her "Memoirs" to the time when Mademoiselle Anne de Bourbon was introduced into society — she herself being then little more than nine years of age — says she used to go twice a week to the *réunions* of the Comtesse de Soissons at the Hôtel de Brissac, where there were music and dancing, and often short plays were performed; but what most amused her and her companion, Mademoiselle de Longueville (the duke's daughter), was to go there ridiculously dressed — "*aussi ridiculement qu'on le pouvait être*," and to laugh at and make grimaces at the company, in spite of the incessant reprimands of their governess. To ensure better behaviour, it appears to have been necessary to separate these two horrid girls; both of whom professed a great dislike to the

Princess de Condé, as well as to her daughter, then the destined stepmother of Mademoiselle de Longueville.

Between stepmother and stepdaughter, so nearly of the same age, no mutual affection ever sprang up; while as to the duke, though he had married the most celebrated beauty of her day, he continued to be one of the train of ardent worshippers who followed the triumphal car of the handsomest and most ignorant woman in France, — Madame de Rohan Montbazon. She was the granddaughter of Varenne, *maître d'hôtel* to Henri IV. The *grandes dames*, therefore, indignant at the number and rank of the slaves who wore her chains, were accustomed to speak contemptuously of her as "the cook's daughter." However, she had married into a branch of the great Rohan family, who claimed kindred with royalty, and one of whose members assumed the arrogant device of

> " Roi, je ne puis,
> Duc, je ne daigne,
> Rohan je suis."

The indifference of the duke does not appear to have affected the young duchess or to have prevented her from fully enjoying the pleasures of the capital. And as by the laws of polite society every gentleman was bound either to be, or to feign to be, in love, and to sigh, "*en amant inoffensif*," at the feet of a mistress, and every lady to have her *"galant et honnête homme," la belle duchesse* had but to select from among her numerous slaves the one she decreed worthy of the honour of attending upon her. She did not affect wit; she wrote no sonnets, but she conversed well, — fluently, gracefully, and easily, and what was rarer still, naturally; a talent highly appreciated and a good deal envied at Rambouillet. It was there she formed that life-long friendship with the Marquise de Sablé, who though scarcely to be classed amongst the writers of the period, originated the fashion of writing *maximes et pensées*. There, too, she became acquainted with the brother and sister De Scudéry, both so unswervingly devoted to her.

But by some writers the Duchesse de Longueville has been represented as admiring, above all things, her own beauty, and as receiving the highest delight she was capable of from the flatteries and homage that beauty procured her. She was a very lovely blonde; a type of beauty that would seem to have been more frequent in those days both in Spain and France than at present. For those exceptionally lovely women, whose charms were so rapturously sung, were all endowed by the poet and the lover with light chestnut or golden hair; eyes blue as the southern skies, forms graceful as the bounding sylph, yet with a modicum of *embon-*

point. The imagination of a lover will doubtless often endow his mistress with charms which ordinary eyes see not; but as regards Madame de Longueville, one is bound to believe from concurrent testimony that she was a truly beautiful woman.

But that scourge of beauty, small-pox, though lying dormant for a time, was ever lurking in the narrow, pestiferous streets of old Paris. Breaking forth suddenly, it swept away its victims by hundreds and thousands, and snatched from the cheek of beauty every trace of its comeliness, leaving only scars and hideousness behind. How it was dreaded, both by the highborn and the lowly! In the year following her marriage, and in the midst of the pleasures and gaieties she now so greatly delighted in, the young and lovely Duchesse de Longueville was smitten by this terrible disease.

CHAPTER XVI.

War with Spain. — Louis's Love of the Camp. — Birth of the Dauphin. — A second Enfant de France. — Le Grand Condé. — Marries Richelieu's Niece. — Morbid Fancies of Louis XIII. — Death of Marie de Médicis. — Sympathy of the People. — Richelieu's failing Health. — Cinq Mars. — Provokes the King's Anger. — His picturesque Appearance. — Un mauvais quart d'heure. — Death of the great Cardinal. — If a great Minister, but a poor Poet.

LOUIS XIII. was at war with Spain, and chiefly because it was the will of his minister, who found in war the gratification of his own ambition, and a means of amusing and controlling the king. Louis's desire to govern for himself often inclined him to break the bonds in which the cardinal held him, and to take the reins of power into his own weak hands. But it was beyond his ability to set himself free, and, considering his character, hardly desirable that he should do so. When, however, he became weary of his favourites, and his yoke lay heavy upon him, the cardinal devised a military promenade, as an effectual method of easing it. Louis XIII. was not without personal bravery; he was a bold huntsman and a fearless rider. He liked the din of the camp, as his father had done, though he was there amongst the cardinal's creatures, and not, as was Henry IV., amongst comrades and friends.

Henry was a rough and hardy soldier, with a lively temper and a winning tongue; poor Louis was a gloomy recluse and a stammerer. But he liked to ride at the head of his troops, and to show himself to his army. It gave him an advantage, he thought, over Philip IV. of Spain, who had never been seen by his soldiers. Except by name, they knew him not at all, while the French troops were frequently favoured with the inspiring sight of their king, as he passed them in review if he never led them to battle. The result of all this warfare, if damaging to Austria and Spain, was even more disastrous to France, — exhausting the finances and depopulating the country.

To talk over the changes and chances of the war, and the plots and intrigues, which Louis could never divest himself of the idea that Anne of Austria took a deep interest, if not a chief part in, he often, by means of the *passe-partout* of his royal prerogative, contrived, in spite of the cardinal's spies and the vigilance of Vincent de Paul, to spend an hour or so at the grating with Mdlle. de La Fayette. Into her sympathizing ear he poured the tale of his military and political hopes and fears, and his complaints and suspicions of his wife. She consoled, comforted, and advised, and brought him for a time to think less unkindly

Louis XIIII.

of the queen; and but for her apathy, Louis might have been constrained to acknowledge that Anne had been unfairly and harshly treated. When, however, to the joy of the nation (who, owing to the weak health of the king, had begun to fear that Gaston might shortly reign over them, and expected no advantage from the change), a son was born to Louis, he refused to take the infant in his arms, and, as was customary, kiss him. And Anne was far more deeply pained by this affront than by all his neglect and indifference.

An astrologer was in waiting in the adjoining room for the announcement of the birth, in order immediately to cast the child's nativity. His prediction of the brilliant destiny of the future Louis XIV. probably helped to soothe the wounded feelings of the mother, who was as firm a believer in the arts of the astrologer, and his power to see into futurity, as she was in the efficacy of the superstitious practices of her church to win the favour of Heaven. The people were not backward in celebrating the birth of the dauphin; and there was a magnificent state christening, at which Mazarin — who was then nuncio extraordinary in France, and high in the favour of Richelieu — held the child for Pope Urban VIII. As the little dauphin lived and throve, and a second son — Philippe, Monsieur — was born within the next two years, Gaston could no longer look to succeed to the throne. The consideration he had hitherto been held in by the many plotters and intriguers against the cardinal minister considerably declined. But there was still a chance of the regency, as it was doubtful whether Louis's experience of the incompetency of his mother to govern the kingdom, and the almost contemptuous opinion he had of the character and abilities of the queen, would not outweigh his hatred of his brother, and lead him, in case of a minority, to appoint him regent.

Gaston, from restlessness of disposition and discontent with the cardinal, who refused him the government of certain provinces he desired, was ever ready to favour any plot or conspiracy against the court and the minister, and to invite others to revolt. But when their schemes were discovered or frustrated, he scrupled not to sacrifice his partizans and friends in order to make his own peace. He possessed personal courage, but his seditious enterprises were as readily abandoned as undertaken, owing to instability of purpose; while those who had supported them were as promptly deserted, from his utter want of honour and moral principle. He was the cause of the execution of the brave and intrepid Montmorenci, and of that of Cinq Mars and De Thou.

The fortune of war had been long unfavourable to France, when, at about this time, a young general of but twenty years of age turned the tide in its favour. The Spaniards laughed at the idea of a beardless boy commanding an army that was to face the veteran troops of Spain, led by a distinguished and experienced general. The boy commander was the young Duc d'Enghien, better known as the Grand Condé. "The art of war," as a French writer has remarked, "seemed to be in him a natural instinct." Other great captains have learned it by degrees, and generally have acquired renown only after experience in the battle-field; but the Grand Condé was born a general, and he was a general that never was beaten. Richelieu had arranged a marriage between the duke and his niece, Mademoiselle de Maillé de Brézé, notwithstanding the objections raised by Madame la Princesse against a union with the family of the man who had sent her brother to the scaffold. The prince, who saw in it the prospect of further enriching his family, had overruled her objections. The bridegroom himself was indifferent, for the bride was not beautiful, and she, having no voice in the matter, became, willingly or unwillingly, Duchesse d'Enghien.

The education of the young duchess — though she was the daughter of a distinguished man of ancient and noble family, the Maréchal de Maillé de Brézé, greatly enriched, too, since Richelieu had governed — had been so entirely neglected, that she could neither read nor write. That she might receive some rudimentary instruction, the duke placed her in the Carmelite convent of St.

Denis, during his absence on a journey to Roussillon, with the king. Before setting out on this journey, the king, who was always tormented by evil suspicions, broke a piece of money with M. de Martigny, almost the only member of his household in whom he had confidence, and enjoined him to keep a careful and constant guard over the two young princes. On no account was he to allow them to be removed, or to be placed under another's supervision, even if he should receive an order to do so under his, the king's, own hand. If evil should seem to threaten them, M. de Martigny was to apprize him of it by sending the half piece of money left with him. The king, however, returned to find that his children were well, and had been in no way molested. What he suspected, or whom he mistrusted, was never known; but he was a prey to these morbid fancies.

There is no greater blot on the memory of Louis XIII. than his treatment of his mother. She had not only vainly solicited permission to return to France, but had been allowed for eleven years to live in great indigence, dependent, in a foreign country, on the sympathy and aid of strangers. She was accustomed, when she would humiliate the king and his minister in the eyes of the friends she met with, to point to her mean dress, soiled and threadbare, and to her miserable rooms, destitute of necessary furniture. In this poverty she died, at Cologne, on the 3rd of July,

1642. She was attended in her last hours by the ecclesiastic Chigi, who became pope under the name of Alexander VII. Asking her "if she forgave De Richelieu?" she replied, "Yes. With all my heart;" but she refused to send him, as Chigi suggested, any pledge to that effect, saying, "*C'est un peu trop.*" She made a will, leaving some small sums to those who had been kind to her, and naming the amount she owed to several persons, all of which she entreated the king not to refuse to pay. Her cross, surrounded with diamonds, and containing a piece of the supposed true cross, she had preserved, she said "*par triste plaisanterie.*" She left it to her daughter Henrietta, wife of Charles I., and, in some respects, more unfortunate than herself.

Rubens had received Marie de Médicis with great kindness, and for some considerable time she was a guest in the house he had built for himself at Cologne. He wrote several letters to the cardinal on her behalf, which were acknowledged by an offer from him of ten thousand pistoles, or louis d'or, for the master's great picture, "The Descent from the Cross." Rubens declined it, preferring, patriotically, that this grand *chef-d'œuvre* should remain in the country of his birth.

The king and his court mourned, in their black and violet robes, for the unfortunate queen of Henry IV., though she had died in lonely poverty and exile. Marie de Médicis, in the days of her grandeur and power, though she sought popularity, did not succeed in acquiring it. But her melancholy fate had caused her follies and her incapacity for governing to be forgotten, and pity and sympathy were felt for her, as a mother harshly treated by her son, and oppressed by the minister who first owed his elevation to her. True, the king had addressed a declaration to the parliament and the governors of the provinces, in which he attempted to justify his own and his minister's conduct towards his mother, — a strange condescension on the part of one who deemed kings so highly placed above the rest of the world, that no remonstrance, no comment on their acts, was permissible to the race of inferior mortals they by divine right reigned over. An accusing conscience probably led him to stoop to excuse himself in the eyes of the people. Nevertheless, they continued to pity poor Marie de Médicis, and to regard her as a victim to the weakness of the king and the ambition of the minister.

Richelieu was himself at that time in failing health; toil and anxiety were telling upon him. For with all his power and implacability, his unfailing prudence, penetration, and energy, he had found it no easy task at once to curb the power of Austria; to subdue the zeal of the Huguenots; to humble the haughty and turbulent spirit of the *noblesse;* to extinguish the liberties and privileges of the people; to control a weak but impatient and fretful monarch, and to thwart the intrigues of his enemies, who aimed at overthrowing his power, and even at taking his life. His constitution was giving way under the incessant mental and physical strain he had for years undergone, to maintain his own power and position while establishing absolute authority in the throne. While lying ill at Avignon, he received confirmation of a conspiracy against him, in which Spain had been asked and had promised to aid. Gaston d'Orléans, the Duc de Bouillon, and Louis's but lately chief favourite, Cinq Mars, were concerned in it. As usual, Gaston not only withdrew when the scheme became impracticable, but gave information that caused the arrest of his associates, and the execution of Cinq Mars and De Thou.

Cinq Mars, who was called Monsieur le Grand, from his office of *grand écuyer* to the king, owed his introduction to the court to Richelieu. He was a mere youth when placed as page in the royal household; but his distinguished air, his vivacity, and many accomplishments soon brought him into notice and great favour. Places of trust and large emoluments of course followed; but this young gentleman disappointed the expectations of his patron. He thought more of amusing himself than of pleasing the king, and did not prove sufficiently pliant for the favourite of a weak monarch. At first his caprices and fancies, his skill in a variety of games then in favour, his haughty airs, his extravagant expenditure, magnificence in dress, and firm belief that his own merits had gained him so much credit with the king, rather amused Louis than displeased him. But Cinq Mars had but little discretion, and too much faith in himself to perceive that his favour was on the decline.

He was with the king at the siege of Perpignan, and accompanied him into the trenches. Without any experience in the art of war, he yet interfered in the military arrangements, and spoke slightingly and jestingly of the operations of the siege. His ill-timed mirth and raillery were resented by the officers, and, worse than all for Cinq Mars, provoked an ebullition of temper in the king, who thought himself a great soldier, and expected others to think, or feign to think, the same. The *badinage* of Cinq Mars was therefore fatal to him.

"*Allez! orgueilleux,*" stammered out the king; "*vous voulez que l'on croie que vous employez une partie de la nuit à régler avec moi les affaires de mon royaume; et vous les passez dans ma garde-robe, à lire des romans avec mes valets de chambre. Allez! Il y a six mois que je vous vomis!*"

Mortified vanity, resentment and thoughtlessness drew poor Cinq Mars into the plot against Richelieu, who was supposed to prompt every act of the king. When arrested and placed in confinement, he believed it to be a mere show of severity towards him, and that he would be speedily released. His apartment not being sufficiently elegant, he was allowed to send for his own furniture, and his costly bed —a most luxurious and sumptuous couch, with hangings of the richest scarlet silk and gold brocade. When he was brought before the Council appointed to try, or rather to condemn him (for the cardinal, though on the very brink of the grave, had already decreed the fate of this vain and thoughtless young man of twenty-four), his appearance excited great interest. He is described as "exceedingly handsome, tall, well-proportioned, and graceful." He wore a *pourpoint*, or vest, of fine Flemish cloth of a pale brown colour, ornamented with gold lace. Over this was thrown a long scarlet cloak, with large and finely chased gold buttons, and his wavy brown hair fell in curls on his shoulders.

When convinced that the proceedings were no mere form, and that it was really intended that his life should pay the forfeit of his folly, he at once resigned himself to his fate and requested to be allowed to see his confessor. To him, he said, "nothing had so much grieved him as to find himself deserted in the hour of misfortune by all whom he had believed to be his friends. I could not have supposed it possible," he exclaimed, "and I learn only now, when too late to profit by it, that the friendships of the court are but dissimulation." When executed he was dressed as above, with the addition of a black Catalonian hat and plume, green silk stockings, and white silk pantaloons, with fine Flemish lace at the knees.

With this charming young cavalier was also executed his friend, the Councillor de Thou, the son of the historian. He had taken no part whatever in the plot, but had disapproved of it entirely. His crime was that, having been made acquainted with it, he did not betray his friend. They embraced before laying their heads on the block, and both met their fate with courage. As the hour appointed for the execution was drawing nigh, the king, looking at his watch, remarked with much satisfaction that Monsieur le Grand "*passait alors un mauvais quart-d'heure*"—this is said to have been the origin of the phrase. Cinq Mars was the lover of Marion Delorme, and would have married her had he lived. His relatives naturally were opposed to it,—his mother especially, who was of a very high family. But he had resolved upon it, being greatly attached to her. This, it has been asserted, was a chief cause of Richelieu's resentment towards Cinq Mars, as he, also, aspired to the good graces of that celebrated courtesan.

But the hand of death was upon the great cardinal; and vengeance being sated, he desired to return to the capital. Accordingly he was borne from Lyons to Paris in a litter, on the shoulders of his guards; a detachment preceding him to make breaches in the walls of the fortified towns on his *route*, that no delay might occur in admitting him, and no unnecessary *détour* lengthen his journey. He declared, on receiving the sacrament, that during the whole course of his ministry "his sole aim had been to secure the prosperity and general good of the state, and to promote the practice of religion." The public voice did not ratify this declaration; rather, the serenity of his deathbed was thought marvellous in one who had sacrificed so many lives to his ambitious views. He died on the 4th of December, 1642, and was buried in the Sorbonne, which he had rebuilt, and where a splendid mausoleum was erected to his memory. The Palais Cardinal, henceforth Palais Royal, he had made a present of to the king three years after its completion, to allay, as was supposed, Louis's dissatisfaction at the splendour of the cardinal's style of living. Besides the palace, he bequeathed to the king the magnificent tapestry he was accustomed to expose on the festival of the Corpus Christi, as well as 500,000 *écus*,— a large sum of money in those days. The royal printing house, the botanical gardens, and many improvements in Paris, were due to Richelieu.

He has been called "the precursor of the French Revolution," and his character and ministry have been variously estimated. But he played too prominent a part in the affairs of France and of Europe for any attempt to be made in these pages to presume to pass judgment upon him. He was the author of several works on politics and religion. The subjects of several plays were also furnished by him to the five authors he employed to write for his theatre, and some part of the verses were from his own pen; but however great he may be considered to have been as a minister, he was certainly a very poor poet.

CHAPTER XVII.

Louis once more is King. — Economy the Order of the Day. — Le Seigneur de Montauron. — Couverts à la Montauron. — Profuse Hospitality. — Corneille and his Patrons. — Death of Louis XIII. — Anne appointed Regent. — Paris at the Death of Louis XIII. — The Cardinal's Improvements. — Oases in the Desert. — Numerous Convents.

FREED from the control of his monitor, Louis again felt as at the death of the Maréchal d'Ancre, when he exclaimed, "*Enfin je suis roi!*" He was now "every inch a king," free to regulate the affairs of his kingdom according to his own notions of good and wise government. First, he sat down and composed an air to the *rondeau* on the death of the cardinal, beginning, "*Il a passé, il a plié bagage;*" then, "*avare reconnu en toutes choses*" — he began his reforms by revoking all pensions granted by the cardinal to indigent men of letters; remarking, as he drew his pen through each name, "*nous n'avons plus affaire à cela.*" He determined also to reduce the expenditure in his household, and to limit it to what was but strictly necessary. A *potage*, therefore, which his *aide-de-camp*, General Coquerel, was accustomed to take every morning, henceforth was to be discontinued, also the biscuits of which M. de la Veillière was in the bad habit of eating too many. Others were found to indulge in such dainties as pastry and preserves, to eat fruit from the king's garden that might have put money into his purse if sold in the markets. Some miscreants, too, had not scrupled when ill, or feigning to be ill, to pamper their appetites with pots of jelly, — thus causing the supply for the king's table to come to an end before the date he had set down for its renewal.

Louis XIII. piqued himself on raising spring vegetables earlier in the season than any other market-gardener. He superintended all gardening operations himself, and allowed none of the early crops to be supplied to his own table or consumed by his household. His green-peas were always the first in the market, and were bought, at any fancy price the king might choose to place on them, by the *maître d'hôtel* of the wealthy Pierre du Puget, Seigneur de Montauron, Conseiller du roi, also Premier Président au Bureau des finances à Montauron. It is proper to give his name and title in full, for he was a most magnificent personage and spent his wealth right royally. His own gardens were chiefly laid out in pleasure-grounds, though a large space reserved for fruit-bearing trees and vegetables produced abundantly. But M. de Montauron kept open house all the year round for princes and *grands seigneurs*, whether at home or called away by the duties of his office. It pleased him, therefore, to have a king for his greengrocer, fruiterer, and vintner (he took the choicest produce of the royal vineyards), to supply the extra needs of his profusely-spread hospitable board.

M. de Montauron was a native of Gascony. His magnificent style of living, his profuse liberality and desire to excel in all things, had gained him the *sobriquet* of "Son Éminence Gascone." So great was his celebrity that shopkeepers named their best and finest goods, whether for the table or for personal wear, "*à la Montauron.*" Richly-embroidered gloves, the finest and most expensive lace kerchiefs or ties, were "*gants, et fichus, à la Montauron,*" a new *calèche*, less cumbrous and more elegant in form, was "*à la Montauron.*" In short, this magnificent Seigneur de Montauron was the leader of fashion, from gloves and fans, hats and feathers, glass, china and silver plate, to the fine bread supplied for his table, which, from its purity and whiteness, was called "*pain à la Montauron.*" The Duc de Montausier, whose establishment was also maintained *sur un grand pied*, had introduced at his table large silver spoons and forks instead of the inconveniently small ones in general use. The idea was immediately turned to account by some one of the loyal retainers of "Son Éminence Gascone;" and a knife of a suitable size being added, they appeared at the daily banquet as "*couverts à la Montauron*," to the admiration of a numerous party of distinguished guests. Speedily they became the fashion; the duke gaining credit as the first to adopt it, while the glory of originating it rested on the brow of the Seigneur de Montauron.

It was esteemed such a piece of good fortune to obtain a place amongst the numerous serving-ing men of the Montauron household, that the *maître d'hôtel* had always a long list of applicants to select from to fill up any vacancy that occurred; and the lucky individual on whom his choice fell readily paid him his customary fee of ten *louis d'or* — a large sum for a *douceur* of that kind in those days. M. de Montauron was no less profuse in aiding the indigent than in entertaining his friends. He gave largely to the charities of Vincent de Paul. Indeed, with such a reputation it was scarcely possible for him to refuse any demand on his bounty, and apparently he had well-filled coffers to draw upon.

He was a pleasant-tempered man and a genial host, and never more delighted than when princes condescended to make themselves as much at home in his house as in their own hôtels. Of those who availed themselves of his hospitality to its fullest extent — to live at free quarters and borrow his money — he was accustomed to say, "*Ils sont sur l'état de ma maison.*" It was his habit, and it was generally understood that it was permitted to him, to *tutoyer* those princely guests and the *grands seigneurs* for whom he provided so sumptuous a table. His *bénédicité* was always an hilarious " *Ça, ça, mes enfants ! rejouissons nous !*" There was also a Mademoiselle de Montauron, a natural daughter but presumptive heiress. She was a handsome girl, educated in the best manner then possible, and treated in all respects *en princesse*. Appropriately, therefore, an Italian prince is said to have been chosen by M. de Montauron to be honoured with her hand and large dowry.

Corneille dedicated his tragedy of "Cinna" to this magnificent Gascon, and in the usual flattering language of the dedicatory epistles of those days, compared him to the "Grand Auguste." De Montauron sent the poet, in return, a purse containing two hundred pistoles, or louis d'or. The king having heard of this liberality, was rather disconcerted when the Duc de Schomberg, on the part of Corneille, requested permission to dedicate to him his tragedy of "Polyeucte." "*Non, non,*" he replied in his stammering way, when confused, "*il n'est pas nécessaire.*"

"Sire," said the duke, "it is not from interested motives that Corneille seeks this honour."

"*Bien, donc bien,*" answered Louis, much relieved, "*il me fera plaisir.*"

The play not being completed until after the king's death, was dedicated to Anne of Austria,

She, also, was not moved to imitate De Montauron's liberality.

Louis XIII. died on the 14th of May, 1643, — the same month, and same day of the month, as Henry IV. was assassinated. He dreaded death, and during his last illness made a solemn vow that if God would be pleased to restore him to health, he would abdicate, as soon as his son should be able to mount and ride a horse, when he would retire to a monastery, and, as a monk, devote the rest of his life to prayer and penitence. But it was evident that his end was approaching, and Vincent de Paul, as his spiritual director, strove to prepare his mind to look with calmness upon it.

Mazarin, who, at the recommendation of Louis XIII., had received the cardinal's hat in 1641, and, on the day following Richelieu's death, had been admitted a member of the supreme council of state, had become from that time devoted to France. Of him the king made choice to be the sole adviser of the queen in ecclesiastical affairs; for he gave her the name of regent, but without power to act independently of a council of regency, the members of which he appointed himself, and who were to remain in office until his successor should be of age. His intention was to perpetuate the state of abasement in which he had for so many years kept his wife and brother. "He said he wished to bridle the queen," to prevent her interference in the government of the country; for, like the meddling of Marie de Médicis, it would lead only to confusion and the upsetting of all order in the state's councils. This testament, surrounding the queen with innumerable limitations and reserves, Mazarin signed, and Louis, with more resignation, then turned his thoughts from earthly things. The queen, in tears, threw herself at his feet. He desired his confessor to raise her, and seemed to signify that she had his forgiveness; but he passed away without any other sign of respect or feeling for her, for he believed as little in her virtue as her capacity.

"The people," says Tallemant, "flocked to the king's funeral, and as full of laughter and merriment as if going to a wedding; while the procession that set out to meet and welcome the queen was like a company of masquers on their way to a *carrousel*. They pitied her," he adds, "because they did not yet know her." But Anne was already invested with absolute authority. Scarcely was the testament of Louis XIII. signed ere it was completely set aside. Mazarin, as he declared, had subscribed to it, notwithstanding its restrictions, for the advantage of the queen, — and a little, no doubt, for his own. The title of regent being conferred on her by the king, she immediately, following the example of Marie de Médicis, appealed to the parliament to confirm it, and, at the same time, to annul the restraints imposed on her. The parliament, whose political influence had for years been as naught, and that would not have dared, in the time of the great cardinal and the king, to raise their voice to express an opinion on any public affair of importance, not only confirmed the title of the queen-regent, but at once cast to the winds all Louis's limitations, and placed in her hands the uncontrolled government of France. They also gratified the Duc d'Orléans by conferring on him the titular office of Lieutenant General of the kingdom.

Paris had outgrown its old limits greatly during the reign of Louis XIII., especially on the north side of the Seine. Any improvements or embellishments it had undergone were due, however, to Marie de Médicis or to Richelieu, for Louis's limited share of power was used to restrict rather than to further the magnificent projects of his minister, who himself was hampered by his incessant wars and their drain on the resources of the country, as well as his want, apparently, of financial ability in the management of the revenues of the state. The bastions extended, at the time of Louis's death, beyond the present enclosure of the Tuileries gardens towards the Place de la Concorde; the new rampart passing along the site of the Rue Royale towards the modern Boulevards de la Madeleine and des Italiens. Indeed, those boulevards, which the ancient rampart afterwards gave place to, mark with tolerable accuracy the extent of old Paris, with its then new quarter — the present Rue de Castiglione, Place Vendôme, Rue de la Paix, and the streets branching off east and west.

The first improvement Richelieu made in Paris was the widening of the Rue de la Ferronnerie, where Henry IV. was assassinated. He also widened the street that bears his name, and built the gate that led out of the city on the side of Montmartre. The longest and finest street was still the Rue St. Antoine. The botanical garden just beyond the monastery of the Assumption, near the present site of the Madeleine, was established by Richelieu's orders. It served then to supply flowering plants for the parterres of the Tuileries gardens. But old Paris, to accommodate its army of useless monks and nuns, was encumbered with large monasteries and convents innumerable; and though many fine hôtels of the *noblesse* were built during the reign, yet their high outer walls, together with the gloomy surroundings of the numerous monastic buildings, and the network of crooked and narrow and filthily dirty streets, formed a *tout ensemble* of the dreariest kind, even by day, but especially when darkness came on.

Yet there were oases of brightness in this desert of gloom, and on sunny spring mornings and moonlight summer evenings, the dirty old city, then one of the chief plague-spots of Europe, might, even in the days of "*triste Louis Treize,*" have been called "gay Paris." Those oases were the Cours de la Reine, and the gardens of the Place Royal, where beauty and fashion loved to disport themselves. Then behind the high walls were large private grounds, where the dwellers in fine hôtels could ramble at their pleasure, or assemble their friends for the garden-parties of the period. But the poor! Ah! it was a fearful place for the poor. It was well for them that even one ecclesiastic was found to teach that it was in the world that God should be served, and not in the convent cells. For Paris, from the rapidly increasing number of its monastic establishments, seemed likely to become a city of convents — abodes of superstition, ignorance, idleness, and vice.

CHAPTER XVIII.

Recovery of the Young Duchess. — She reappears in the Beau Monde. — Chapelain's "Pucelle." — The Duchess's Opinion. — La Guirlande de Julie. — Tallemant des Réaux. — Les "Historiettes." — Nicholas Rambouillet. — Madame de la Sablière. — La Haute Volée and the Financier. — Funeste Distraction.

THE small-pox had been merciful to the brilliant beauty of the young Duchesse de Longueville. The dreaded disease, which appears to have been more generally in France than elsewhere a virulent and lingering one, sinking deep into the skin, scarring and indenting the face frightfully, had, in her case, passed off in a comparatively slight attack. The anxious fears of her family for her life and her beauty; her own trembling anticipations of recovering but to find her career of conquest cut short at its outset, were dispelled as the traces of the malady gradually left her. The face resumed its smoothness and fairness, and after a season of retirement at Chantilly, she reappeared, we are told, in the *beau monde*, "*dans tout l'éclat de sa beauté*" — its freshness and brightness undiminished. She had grown taller during her absence from society; and, while retaining her *embonpoint*, had lost her extremely girlish air, and thus, as her admirers considered, had gained in attractiveness.

Of the *salons* of the hôtels of the *noblesse*, then thrown open to general society in imitation of the Hôtel de Rambouillet, the *salon bleu* of the latter was most frequently graced by the presence of the young duchess. She herself did not pretend to the reputation of a *bel esprit* — she was content to shine as a beauty. She contributed no *bouts rimés* when *bouts rimés* formed the pastime of the evening; she wrote no sonnets; she took no part in the discussions on the suppression of old words and the coining of new ones; on the omission of the superfluous "*s*," and the desirableness of transforming, in certain combinations, the "*u*" into "*v*." But she liked to hear all those things, and, being indolently disposed, to hear them at her ease, while reclining on a sofa, charmingly dressed, and with the five or six "*honnêtes hommes — amants inoffensifs*," who were permitted to sigh at her feet, grouped around her. Thus she both improved her mind and amused herself without too much fatigue or excitement, the energy of character she afterwards displayed then lying dormant and unsuspected in her. Her preference for Rambouillet was, in a great measure, owing to the marquis having been Gouverneur to Monsieur le Prince, her father, and that the interest taken by the marquis and marquise in him and his young wife, when flying from Henry's mad pursuit of the princess, was now continued to their children.

The Duchesse de Longueville was regarded at Rambouillet almost as a daughter of the house, and she felt that when there she was to make herself at home, and she did so thoroughly. There she heard "Cinna" and "Polyeucte" read, Calprenède's romances, and the plays of Georges de Scudéry. Also Chapelain's famous "Pucelle," half of which was pushed by his friends through several editions. The remaining six books were left in MS.; for patience could endure no more, notwithstanding the praises of Bishop Huet, and the influence brought to bear to obtain popularity for it. Every one, at its first reading, desired to dissemble his real feeling, from consideration to a man of much erudition, who had fallen into the error of believing himself a poet, and to say something which should not be exactly praise of his melancholy production, yet not altogether disapproval. The duchess, on this occasion, being pressed for her opinion, said, "*Sans doute, c'était un très beau poème, mais aussi très ennuyeux.*"

But at this time (1641) the society of Rambouillet was greatly interested in an offering which the Duc de Montausier was preparing for presentation to Julie d'Angennes. That faithful swain had now been for ten years her constant lover. To mark this epoch in the long course of their true love, which, as usual, did not run smooth (for "it stood upon the choice of friends," who would have none of a Huguenot), the duke proposed to offer his Julie a garland, which should express, emblematically, all the virtues he believed her possessed of, and the love and admiration he felt for her. Eighteen flowers were arranged in a garland, and painted on vellum, in folio, by Robertet, the most celebrated flower-painter of the day.

Eighteen of her poet friends, of whom the duke, inspired by the Muses for the occasion, was one, described in a madrigal the sentiments which each flower of the garland was supposed to represent; the flowers that composed it being also painted separately, each on a distinct page, and each poet's contribution written under the emblematic blossom to which it related. The writing was in the hand of the celebrated caligraphist, Jarry. Both the painting and writing are said to have been exquisite, and the binding of the volume superb. The duke named his offering "La Guirlande de Julie." *

* The superb volume presented by the lover to his mistress, and so celebrated as "La Guirlande de Julie," passed from the family, after the death of the duke and the duchess, into the hands of the Abbé Rothélin. From him it descended to M. de Rose, and was then bought by the Duc de la Vallière, at the sale of whose property, towards the end of the last century, it was sold (Roederer's "Mémoires pour servir") for 14,510 francs. The editor of the "Historiettes" says it is still in the possession of the family of the Duc d'Uzès, the great grandson of the Duc de la Vallière. A copy was published in 1784, by Didot, of Paris. Another in 1824, by Amoreaux, of Montpelier.

The poetic effusions were of course of unequal merit. Voiture, Scudéry, and Benserade, were amongst the contributors. Victor Cousin gives the madrigal of the lily by Tallemant des Réaux; his production is as follows:—

MADRIGAL SUR LA FLEUR DU LIS.

A MDLLE. JULIE D'ANGENNES DE RAMBOUILLET.

"Devant vous je perds la victoire,
  Que ma blancheur me fit donner;
 Et ne prétends plus d'autre gloire
  Que celle de vous couronner.

"Le ciel, par un honneur insigne,
  Fit choix de moi seul autrefois,
 Comme de la fleur la plus digne,
  Pour faire un présent à nos rois.

"Mais si j'obtenais mon requête,
  Mon sort serait plus glorieux,
 D'être monté sur votre tête
  Que d'être descendu des cieux." *

Gèdèon Tallemant des Réaux, who has frequently been confounded with his brother, the Academician, François Tallemant, and sometimes with his nephew, Paul Tallemant, also of the French Academy, was so constant a frequenter of the Hôtel de Rambouillet that he has been called "the historian of the famous

---

* This is an allusion to the legend which ascribes the adoption of the lily as the emblem of France by one of its saintly kings to its having descended upon him from heaven. It is singular that an emblem of purity should also have been employed as a brand of disgrace for certain malefactors.

Hôtel," and "the Brantôme of the seventeenth century." He wrote for his own amusement, and with unsparing severity satirized his contemporaries, and ridiculed and censured the manners of the age.

"*Les 'Historiettes,'*" says Victor Cousin, "*désenchantent du passé, parcequ'elles sont, avec quelque peu d'exaggération, vraies.*"

Their publication is recent, compared with that of other memoirs of the same period. The existence of the MS. was unknown for a considerable time, and its authenticity at first doubted. The "Historiettes" afford some interesting information respecting the Marquise de Rambouillet and her circle; otherwise, as is much to be regretted, his descriptions of society, like those of too many of the writers of that day, are generally utterly repelling, from their extreme coarseness. It would seem from his allusions to other writings, that he was preparing, or had completed, memoirs of Anne of Austria, and of Cardinal Mazarin; but his family either suppressed them or neglected to preserve the MSS.

He was on terms of intimate friendship with the marquise to the end of her life. Though wealthy, learned, and witty, he was considered by the grandees of the *salon bleu* to be a man of little pretension — one who knew his place — while, in fact, he was observing them very closely, and mentally taking copious notes for his "Historiettes." His family, originally of the *bourgeois* class, had been for a generation or two ennobled; but Tallemant, having married the daughter of the rich banker, Nicholas Rambouillet, had to descend a step of the social ladder, and take rank with his wife's father as "*un homme de finance.*" The nobles of the period, to mark their contempt for the wealthy financiers, were accustomed to call them "*partisans,*" a term applied to those who farmed the king's revenue, and sometimes "*maltôtiers*" or tax-gatherers, being a degree more contemptuous. His own means were ample, and his wife, who was also his first cousin, had a very large fortune. He had asked her in marriage when she was but eleven and a half years old, and the parents approving, they were betrothed, the marriage taking place two years after.

Her father was the Rambouillet who built the fine mansion at the village of Neuilly with the celebrated gardens, to which the name of "la folie Rambouillet" was given. He and his wife received there all the wealthy *haute bourgeoisie*, with a fair proportion of the *beau monde* of the Marais, and a sprinkling of the *noblesse*. The most distinguished of "the men of the gown, men of the sword, and men of letters," might be met at his table, and ladies of high fashion did not disdain to grace the *salon* of the rich banker's wife. The banker's son had some reputation as a poet; his wife, Madame Rambouillet de la Sablière, was a poetess of renown in her day; she is celebrated in the *chansonnettes* of La Fontaine, and the madrigals of the Marquis de la Fare. The marquis was the *cicisbeo* or "*galant et honnête homme*" of the poetess; but he was so much addicted to gambling, one of the great vices of the period, that the game then most in vogue, *bassette*, had almost as much of his time and devotion as the lady. This, according to the chivalric notions then prevalent, was deemed an infidelity, and Madame de la Sablière took it so much to heart, that disdaining either to reproach her faithless knight, or to seek an explanation from him, "she, *sans éclat*, retired to a convent, and devoted the rest of her life to the pious duty of nursing Vincent de Paul's sick folk in the Hôpital des Incurables." Whether the lady's husband approved of this step is not recorded, but he probably was too fully occupied in composing verses, in his quality of poet, shepherd, or knight, to some Chloe or Arthenice, to bestow time or thought on the matter.

But notwithstanding his literary and wealthy connections, his own affluent circumstances, culture and high character, as well as the fact that his sister and both brothers retained their position of nobles, Tallemant des Réaux had sometimes mortifying slights to endure in the aristocratic *salons* he frequented. It was understood that in the *salons* of the Marquise de Rambouillet talent, mental culture and moral worth were regarded as the highest distinctions. But there was a courtly element in the society that thought otherwise, and gave birth and its honours and privileges the first place. Personal merit and education were then but lightly regarded by those who, generally speaking, possessed little of either, and large fortunes certainly did not command the consideration, much less the homage, paid to mere wealth in these days.

Dancing was then so much the rage that it must have been mortifying to a man of Tallemant's position when the lady he sought for his partner, if she did not absolutely refuse him, scarcely deigned to speak to him, or to reply when he addressed her; for ladies of noble birth did not willingly dance with the financiers unless they wished to borrow money of them, or get advances on their jewels to pay their gambling debts. Tallemant des Réaux was the intimate and confidential friend of the eloquent Olivier Patru; the severe Duc de Montausier also valued him highly, and with the whole of the Rambouillet family he maintained the closest ties of friendship. For the rest, he took ample vengeance for all slights, in his "Historiettes," and wrote many a witty couplet of which the theme was "*messieurs les plumets*" (the courtiers), to whose use and adornment white plumes and red heels were sacred.

He has been accused of attempting to disparage the memory of Henry IV. He says, " he was naturally inclined to theft, and would probably have been hanged had he not been a king." That he was, in fact, afflicted too often with a "*funeste distraction*" that led to his appropriating, or endeavouring to appropriate what did not belong to him. It has been supposed that allusion was intended to Henry's *amours*.

CHAPTER XIX.

La Bonne Régence. — Exiles recalled; Captives set Free. — The Bishop of Beauvais. — The Duc de Beaufort. — Cardinal Mazarin. — His affected Humility. — Indolence of the Queen-Regent. — Evenings at Court. — The Wily and "Beau Cardinal." — Laurels and Bays. — Voiture, a Royal Favourite. — An Impromptu.

"J'AI vu le bon temps de la bonne régence," sang Saint Evremond in his latter years, and so promisingly did the regency of Anne of Austria begin, that "*une bonne régence*" was the hope and expectation of all classes. Anne had been oppressed and humiliated, and, as some thought, maligned by her gloomy, suspicious husband and his despotic and implacable minister. And the people who had feared the latter and hated both him and the king, rejoiced with her that she, as well as themselves, was freed from their tyrannous yoke. Anne, too, was all smiles and graciousness. The humbled and dispersed *gentilshommes*, or *petite noblesse*, returned to the court to profit by the new order of things, for nothing was refused, and pensions and places were to be had for asking. The banished offenders were welcomed back to their country. Prison doors were thrown open, and amongst other of Richelieu's captives, the Maréchal de Bassompierre, after twelve years of seclusion in the Bastille, regained his liberty and confiscated property. He was even offered the post of governor to the young king; but he declined the honour, alleging his unfitness for so important a charge on account of age and infirmities.

When La Porte, whose ingenuity had saved the reputation of Anne of Austria, and whose fidelity to her was unshaken by imprisonment and Richelieu's menaces of death, appeared before her as one of the liberated captives, she exclaimed publicly: "*Voilà ce pauvre garçon qui a tant souffert pour moi et à qui je dois tout ce que je suis à présent.*" Anne gave him 100,000 livres to buy the place of premier valet de chambre to the young king. But La Porte was disappointed in his expectation of being admitted to the confidence of his royal mistress as a reward for past faithful services. Possessed of the secrets of her early life, he now warned her that loss of public favour would be the consequence of too great a familiarity of manner in her relations with Mazarin.

The queen-regent, however, chose for her minister the Bishop of Beauvais, but was believed to be much under the influence of a sentimental friendship she entertained for the Duc de Beaufort, the son of César Duc de Vendôme. The bishop — "*idiot des idiots,*" as he was termed — seems to have been chosen for his want of every quality a minister should possess, in order to afford a pretext for raising Mazarin to power. He was greatly disliked by the people, but favourably regarded, it had been suspected, even before Louis's death, by the queen. Beauvais's first use of ministerial power was to inform the Dutch that they must not expect to continue in alliance with France unless they became converted to her religion. Even the bigoted queen felt shocked that such a pretension should have been put forth in her name.

The Vendôme family — always a popular one — was then even more so than usual, owing to the rebuffs, the humiliations and disgrace they and their partizans had undergone at the hands of Richelieu. The Duc de Beaufort had taken a fancy to govern the kingdom; it therefore seemed probable that the bishop would be succeeded by a minister no less incompetent, and infinitely more flighty than himself. The duke played the gallant with great assiduity, and the queen received his attentions with very marked favour. She was still by no means averse to a little flirtation — "gallantry and devotion went hand-in-hand with her." The bishop's imbecility, the queen's excessive indolence, and the distrust she had of her own capacity to conduct affairs of state, made it absolutely necessary that she should change her minister. A great coolness had, however, been observed suddenly to occur in her manner towards Beaufort. She had discovered that he was playing the passionate lover to the beautiful Madame de Montbazon, and that, while he pretended to have eyes only for his sovereign, he was assuring that lady — who had half or more of the *grands seigneurs* of the court sighing at her feet — that his devotion to the mother of his king was solely due to political motives.

Beaufort had been accustomed to spend not only hours, but whole days with the queen, amusing her greatly with his lively conversation and by his gaiety of temper. But idle as she was in every sense — refusing even to undergo the mental fatigue of making herself acquainted with the concerns of the government, or to be troubled to express any will of her own in such matters — she could be haughty and passionate where her feelings were interested. The supple and docile Cardinal Mazarin, by his complaisant and insinuating manners, his engaging conversation, and not unpleasing personal appearance, had already won her favour, and it is probable that she would sooner have relieved herself of the burden of absolute power, which she found so overwhelming, and placed it in his hands, had she not feared to rouse the resentment of her friends.

All who had taken her part, all who had plotted and suffered with her, detested the memory and the political maxims of Richelieu. They abhorred all who had been favoured and raised to office by him, but none did they abhor so much as Mazarin, whom Louis XIII. had made chief of the cabinet on Richelieu's death. Mazarin was aware of the strong prejudice existing against him. He affected to be about to retire from France — "the cabal that opposed him being too powerful a one to be resisted" — and to take up his residence in Italy. But Anne, irritated by the conduct of Beaufort, and sinking under the magnitude of the task she had undertaken, dismissed the incompetent Beauvais, and called in the aid of Mazarin. Unlike Richelieu, Mazarin in manner was gentle, gracious and benignant; he managed affairs very ably, and, by much tact and ductility, gained over the Duke of Orléans, Monsieur le Prince, and others who had supported the queen, but hitherto had been opposed to him.

At first he affected no state, but was as modest in manner and simple in his mode of living as Richelieu had been haughty and overbearing, profuse and luxurious. He not only refused an escort of guards, and forbore to assert — as his arrogant predecessor had done — his right to take the *pas* of the princes, but lamented that his dignity of cardinal forbade him to humble himself to the extent he desired. Soon he became *chef du conseil*, which necessitated *les petits conseils* — long *tête-à-tête* conferences with the queen in the evening, idle gossip or petty intrigue that amused her — for into the business or cares of state she would not enter, and all real authority she gave up to Mazarin absolutely. And for a time everything went well; D'Enghien, Turenne and Gaston d'Orléans fought successfully the battles of the country; the queen passed her time in a monotonous round of dreary amusements, and spent half the day in her bed. The other half was occupied in praying in her oratory, combing her hair, displaying — for adoration — her beautiful hands, and regaling a rather large appetite with savoury dishes and delicacies, for the fragments of which it amused her much to see her bevy of ladies scramble; she laughing still more heartily when — as not unfrequently happened — the servants entered and forcibly bore away for their own table the yet unappropriated scraps of the feast.

This "*grande reine*" never read, — reading was an accomplishment she did not excel in, — and her mental indolence was so excessive that she was incapable of sufficiently sustaining attention to derive either amusement or instruction from the reading of others. She was profoundly ignorant of everything but the etiquette and forms of the court, its scandals, gossip, and intrigue. She was fond of the play, and, after the feast, that was her usual amusement. During her first year of widowhood she sat behind a curtain, concealed from view, that she might seem to respect established customs, while making no sacrifice to them of her inclinations. After the play, there was "*petit conseil*" with the cardinal. If it did not take up too much of the evening, "*elle tenait cercle*," for a short time only. These receptions being fatiguing to her, were rarely numerously attended. If perchance they were, she bade an early good-night to the company, and withdrew to her oratory to pray. At eleven she took supper, and the ladies ate what she left. Afterwards, the night being fine, she walked with a party of her ladies and gentlemen in the gardens of her palace (the Palais Royal), where she would remain for two or more hours after midnight; then home to bed, her ladies gossiping with her in her *ruelle* until her royal eyes were closed in sleep. That devoutly wished-for moment having arrived, they stole softly out of her chamber, respited — poor creatures — from their slavery for a few short hours.

Thus, *doucement, doucement*, and with the same precision as the hands of a clock point to the hour and travel round it, did the inane life of Anne of Austria flow on for some years, knowing no change except such variety in the daily programme as a journey to St. Germain or Fontainebleau necessitated. And doubtless she was happy. She was incapable of friendship as regarded her own sex, and very coldly received Madame de Hautefort — then Duchesse de Schomberg — and Madame de Chévreuse, who had risked much to serve her when, rightly or wrongly, she was suspected and contemned by her husband. "Her Spanish nature needed," says Victor Cousin, respect and homage after having been so long oppressed." The wily and "*beau cardinal*" perceived this, also that her weakness would prove strength to him, and afford the support he needed to carry out his own ends — the acquirement of power, and especially of riches, in a country where he was a stranger and surrounded by rivals and enemies. He threw himself at her feet; being well versed in all the seductive arts then termed "Italian gallantry" — for cardinal though he was, Mazarin was scarcely a priest — and he gained her heart. Master of that, her poor weak mind found relief and comfort in submission to his stronger one. In her name "*Son éminence deuxième*" governed the kingdom, and feathered luxuriously a nest for himself and the tribe of Martinozzi and Mancini.

Meanwhile, laurel wreaths in abundance had been gained by the military heroes of France, but no real advantage for the kingdom, which, "in the midst of apparent prosperity, really stood on the very verge of ruin." The people, the parliament, and the *noblesse*, though greatly dissatisfied with the queen's choice of a minister, were at first comparatively passive under the benign rule of the cardinal. But discontents arose; then came resistance and turbulence, followed by the romantic episode of the Fronde; "*la guerre burlesque*," as it has been termed, though a disastrous civil war while it lasted, and detrimental in its results to the liberties of the people.

There was a tendency in society during the first years of the regency towards a fusion of classes, an undoing of the work begun by Richelieu, whose aim was to keep them distinct, and to mark their gradations by special costumes. But after the establishment of the Académie Française — although a few mediocre verses sufficed often to gain a *fauteuil* there — men of letters rose in the social scale, and the pedestal from which all who wore the helmet and sword had hitherto looked down on the men of the pen, on the magistracy and other professions, was somewhat lowered. The queen showed especial favour to Voiture, who used great freedom of speech when addressing her. But as his *bons mots* and *impromptus* were always complimentary or amusing, she smiled very graciously upon him, and gave him so many places and sinecure offices that Voiture became "*un personnage*." He placed the *de* before his name, lost his genial humour, and was so irascible that he could not endure the slightest contradiction, or opposition to his whims. The income he derived from his various posts, though a very large one, did not suffice to pay his heavy gambling debts and support the extravagant and licentious mode of life he adopted when the sun of royal favour shone upon him.

The queen, taking one day an airing in her *calèche*, perceived Voiture reclining against a tree, apparently in profound meditation. "*Ah! voilà M. de Voiture,*" she exclaimed. "*A quoi donc, pensait-il?*" Voiture was no doubt studying an *impromptu*, with no idea, of course, that the queen was driving in that direction. He advanced, and bowing low answered her inquiry as follows:

> "Je pensais si le cardinal,
> J'entends celui de la Valette,
> Pouvais voir l'éclat sans égal
> Dans lequel maintenant vous êtes;
> J'entends celui de la beauté;
> Car auprès je n'estime guère,
> Cela soit dit sans vous déplaire
> Tout l'éclat de la majesté."

"*Fort bien dit, Monsieur de Voiture,*" said the queen laughingly, as she drove off. Such were the freedoms she permitted, and which her favourites often presumed upon.

CHAPTER XX.

War with Spain continued.— Rocroi, Thionville and Cirq.— Public Rejoicings and Fêtes. — Silly Practical Jokes.— The Young Hero and his Family.— Portrait of the Hero.— M. de Feuquières' Protégé. — An appropriate Text. — A Sermon at Rambouillet. — Début of a great Orator. — Un Charmant Homme. — A Fashionable Abbé. — The Abbé foresees a Rival. — The Abbé attempts a Sermon. — Interrupted by a Nervous Lady. — The Congregation disperses.

ANNE OF AUSTRIA, fond of Spain and much attached to her brother, Philip IV., was yet compelled to continue the Spanish war which Richelieu had begun in 1635, and persisted in, though it was difficult to define what was his object beyond making himself necessary to the king. However, on the death of Louis XIII., an order was despatched to the young Duc d'Enghien desiring him to desist from hazarding the battle he was preparing to offer the Spaniards before Rocroi. But the ardour of the duke determined him to disobey the order, and success justified his disobedience. The French arms for more than a hundred years had not gained so brilliant a victory as that of the battle of Rocroi. The triumphs of Henry IV. were little more than those of a guerilla chief leading bands of ill-disciplined troops in time of civil war. But Rocroi was a signal victory gained over the Spanish army, and the duke with the whole of the French troops knelt on the battle-field to thank God for it.

The young hero followed up his success by the siege of Thionville and of Cirq, and took both these towns. He drove the Germans across the Rhine, and followed them for three successive days; he attacked the Spanish General Merci, who was encamped before Fribourg, and throwing his marshal's *bâton* into the intrenchments, marched at the head of his regiment, sword in hand, to regain it. On the fourth day Merci decamped, and Philipsbourg and Mayence surrendered to the duke. Marshals Grammont and Turenne served under him. These distinguished commanders were left in charge of the army, and the duke returned to Paris, where *fêtes* and rewards and the acclamations of all classes of the people awaited him.

The colours taken in battle and other trophies of the war were displayed in the grand saloons of the Hôtel de Condé,* before their removal to Notre Dame. Monsieur le Prince, who was the president of Anne's council of regency, urged

---

* The Hôtel de Condé stood on the site of the present Théâtre de l'Odéon.

with the avidity of avarice his son's claims on the state, while the princess, always proud and haughty, so magnified the deeds of the youthful conqueror, that she seemed to think the crown of Spain should be placed on his brow. There were also great rejoicings at Rambouillet; for the young Count de Pisani had distinguished himself in the regiment of De Conti, which had been led by the duke and had been first in the trenches at Fribourg. An allegorical *fête* was prepared in the park of the Rochers de Rambouillet, and, as was the taste of the day, Julie and her sister, and a train of young ladies, dressed as nymphs, welcomed him to a Temple of Fame erected for the occasion, and where in songs and dances they celebrated the hero of the hour and his companions in arms.

These entertainments were followed by a grand supper, and a good many silly practical jokes — such as forcing on Voiture and other of the guests dishes which they were known to dislike; sewing up their vests or coats, and persuading the owners that something deranging to health must have happened to them — vulgarity which contrasts very strongly with the rather stilted tone of refinement, the intellectual pursuits, the strict etiquette, and chivalric manners of the famous *salon bleu*. Such amusements were the yet lingering traces of the coarse mirth that prevailed in the court of Henry IV. and

Marie de Médicis. But it is surprising to meet with them at the Hôtel de Rambouillet; as disgust at the grossness and boisterous hilarity of the court had driven the marquise to forsake it in her early years, and to form for herself a society apart.* We are told by Tallemant that even with the marquis himself, "*elle vivait un peu trop en cérémonie*," and the same authority ascribes the buffoonery we occasionally hear of at Rambouillet to Voiture, who was no great favourite with him, but whom he describes as "*le père de l'ingénieuse badinerie.*" Voiture, who had a superabundance of animal spirits, may therefore be supposed to have introduced these pranks — for which indeed he often underwent unpleasant, if silly chastisements; but for his liveliness and wit he was not only tolerated but courted and flattered.

Very different, however, from the boyish freaks of Voiture, the academical discussions, the songs and dances and madrigals of the ladies, and the Italian sonnets for which Ménage was then famous, were the entertainments that were sometimes unexpectedly offered to the *habitués* of the *salon bleu*. One such occurred on an evening when a

---

* Courtiers frequented the *salons* of the marquise, but her abhorrence of Louis XIII. was so great that she could never be induced to attend the few *ballets* and *fêtes* which the parsimony of the king permitted. Julie d'Angennes used sometimes to say, "*J'ai peur que l'aversion que ma mère a pour le roi ne la fisse damner.*"

very large and distinguished party had assembled; for the Duc d'Enghien was there, and just then wherever the young hero was known to be, there thronged the *beau monde*, to compliment and flatter, and some even to look at him. For he had burst upon the world as a great general when it was supposed that he had gone to the wars but to take his "*baptême de feu*" under the surveillance of the Maréchal de l'Hôpital. With the duke was the Prince de Conti — his brother, and three years his junior; both were in close attendance on their brilliant sister, to whom they were devotedly attached. Monsieur le Prince and Madame la Princesse were also present to enjoy the triumph of their son and daughter, and with them was the young Duchess d'Enghien — the least considered of the group, a quiet little person, "*sans esprit*," whose husband was distractedly in love with Mademoiselle de Vigeau.

All the beauty of the Condé family was possessed by the princess and her daughter. Madame de Motteville describes the duke as having "a long, thin, and ill-shaped face, an aquiline nose, lively blue eyes, and a haughty expression of countenance, a large and very disagreeable mouth with projecting teeth, yet with something grand and proud in his face, bearing a resemblance to the eagle. To look well," she says, "he should have been more carefully dressed, curled and powdered." He was not above the middle height.

His figure was good, and "though he expressed some contempt for dancing, he danced well," madame says, "and with a very agreeable air." The Prince de Conti was a little humpbacked youth.

But while young Mars and his sister Venus were graciously acknowledging the congratulatory speeches, the profound homage, the eager recognitions that met them on all sides, the Marquis de Feuquières entered the *salon* accompanied by a youth of sixteen or seventeen wearing the dress of an *abbé*. On presenting him to Madame de Rambouillet as a young friend in whom he was much interested, he mentioned that he had chosen and already entered upon an ecclesiastical career, from having an extraordinary facility for extemporaneous speaking, and giving promise of becoming a great preacher. This being whispered about, a general desire was expressed to hear a sermon from this youth, the subject of which should be determined by putting some texts in a bag, and the first that came to hand presented to him. Some objection was taken to the proposal by Madame de Rambouillet — a sermon in a *salon!* — a *salon* where throughout the evening sonnets had been sung or recited in praise of military glory; where Voiture had but just concluded a complimentary address in verse (impromptu of course) in honour of the hero of the day. That it should be followed by a sermon appeared to her a startling incongruity.

But the company generally was of a different opinion, and the young duke also expressing a wish to hear the sermon if Monsieur l'Abbé himself did not object to preach it, the marquise gave way, remarking only that it was very near midnight. This objection being also overruled, and the young *abbé* and his friend assenting to the request of the company, the ladies laid aside their coquettish airs and graces — which they could readily do, being accustomed to go to mass before dressing for a ball or on leaving one *fête* to fill up the interval between that and another — and arranged their faces, after a few sly smiles and glances at their cavaliers, for the sermon. At the further end of the suite of *salons* was a kind of daïs, or raised floor, on which stood the spinet, which was removed, that the young *abbé* might with better effect speak to his brilliant congregation, and be also better heard and seen by them from a slight elevation. The text was selected as proposed. A lady drew forth a slip of paper and presented it to the preacher — "Vanity of vanities; all is vanity." The young man read it, then glanced with a peculiar smile on the beplumed and bejewelled *grandes dames* and their cavaliers, who were seating themselves in the chairs that had been arranged in a wide half-circle round the daïs.

Chance had supplied an appropriate text. The young preacher was accorded a quarter of an hour for preparation, which he declined. Some of the more frivolous of the company scarcely could suppress laughter, as he stepped on the daïs. But the deep, calm, grave voice of the young man, as in simple but eloquent words he pronounced the exordium, soon commanded attention. "Attention became interest; the *salon* was forgotten, and the 'Ave Maria' said as devoutly as in Notre Dame." He then proceeded to unfold before them all the scenes of the great drama of life, "*Qu'est-ce que la vie? — qu'est-ce que l'homme?*" etc. One would not venture to follow him through the different parts of his sermon, even had the discourse been preserved. It is said to have been a long one, but its length was not regarded; for the preacher, wrapped in his subject, carried his auditors with him, as he spoke of the fleeting things of earth, and of death, and the tomb; then, turning from the sepulchre, pointed to heaven and the glories of eternity.

The profound silence that had reigned throughout the discourse continued even for a few minutes after the preacher had concluded, so deep was the impression he had made. Pulpit eloquence was then almost unknown. His poetic fervour and powerful words had fallen on ears accustomed to the dryness and pedantry with which the truths of religion were then invariably set forth. The great preachers of the seventeenth century had not yet appeared. The first of them

Bossuet

was heard that night in the *salons* of Rambouillet. M. de Feuquières hastened to embrace his *protégé*, and the company gathered round him to express their admiration and thanks. No one had asked his name, and, in truth, no one, until this triumph was achieved, had cared to know it. It was but a plebeian one, and had served, with his then provincial air, for a poor jest to the idle young nobles who were supposed to be studying at the college of Navarre, where he was himself a student, lately arrived from Dijon.

The praises so lavishly heaped upon him he acknowledged merely by a bow. He was not insensible to them, for, doubtless, he was ambitious. Had he been but lightly appreciated, he would have felt wounded and abashed; but his success had surpassed even his own expectations, and he stood silent, almost alarmed, at such sudden renown. The Duc d'Enghien, pressing the young man's hand, said, "*Monsieur le prédicateur, pourrait-on savoir votre nom?*" "Bossuet,* *Monseigneur*," he replied. Voiture, who was standing by, as he smiled on the youthful orator, drew forth his watch, and, with an affected start at the

---

* "Bossuet," signifying an ox accustomed to the plough, was a constant theme for jest with the fellow-students of the young preacher. As he never took any part in their recreations, and had scarcely ever been seen to smile, he was not popular among them. He thirsted for distinction, for glory, and this "thunderer of the Church" was a professor while yet but a scholar — a prelate while yet a subdeacon.

lateness of the hour, declared that he had "never before heard preaching so early, or so late."

There was, however, one listener into whose heart the eloquence of the young preacher sent a sharp pang of jealousy. He was a fashionable *abbé*, "*un joli homme, un charmant homme*," with a silky moustache and long wavy hair, apparently a young man of some eight and twenty years. He had delicate hands, and was almost as proud of them as Anne of Austria was of hers (hands which, according to Madame de Motteville, had "received the homage of Europe"). But this gay *abbé* was verging on his fortieth year, notwithstanding his youthful appearance, which was the satisfactory result of the time and pains he expended on his *toilette*. He was an immense favourite with the ladies, and one of the most assiduous frequenters of the Hôtel de Rambouillet. There was ease and elegance in his manners, and he was a pattern of gallantry, deeming his character of *abbé* and Chanoine of Bayeux not incompatible with the sentimental duties and chivalric title of "*galant et honnête homme*." He held the office of almoner to the young king, and was a preacher at the Louvre. He had a pension of three thousand crowns, and many unconsidered trifles besides. He was known, very well known, in his day, as M. l'Abbé Cotin. Molière and Boileau have handed down to posterity his name, and the follies ascribed to him.

When the company rose to congratulate the young preacher, the Abbé Cotin slipped, unperceived, out of the *salon*. He would not, he could not, join the chorus of praise, and it was gall and wormwood to him to listen to it. He felt that it was praise not undeserved, but gained by an effort far beyond his own slender abilities to achieve. Yet he was a member of the Academy, learned in Hebrew and Greek, and a preacher whom the ladies flocked to hear. But the Abbé Cotin was especially the delight of the *salons;* he excelled in the fashionable literary accomplishment of saying and writing pretty nothings in verse. His social reputation was fatal to him as a preacher; for, with a view of pleasing his fair friends, his sermons were composed of pretty platitudes and soft, honeyed phrases. There was no vigour, no force, in them; nothing to prick the conscience, or ruffle the self-complacency of the elegant congregation he addressed weekly in the chapel of the Louvre.

The *abbé* saw in the young preacher the promise of a great orator, and a formidable rival. When he returned to the Hôtel on the following evening the conversation fell chiefly on the extraordinary talent of young Bossuet for extemporary preaching. "What a flow of words! What fluency and distinctness of utterance! What force in his diction, and yet how polished!" Rambouillet itself could detect no flaw in it. "Was not the Abbé

Cotin charmed with the fervour, the piety, the impressiveness of this talented and promising youth?" 'T is la belle Duchesse de Longueville who inquires, and insists on having the opinion of the *abbé* to confirm her own. He smiles, shrugs his shoulders, caresses his moustache, and turns the conversation. In vain; the duchess returns to the subject. "*Eh bien, Monsieur l'Abbé?*" Very sententiously he replies, "The young man *recited* remarkably well."

"Recited!" is echoed in tones of surprise from one end of the *salon* to the other. "Recited," repeats the *abbé*, more emphatically than before; then proceeds to tell his astonished listeners that it was no sermon at all, and to explain to them how a sermon, according to the prescribed forms, should be constructed.

"Monsieur l'Abbé, give us a sermon yourself," said Corneille. The *abbé* dislikes Corneille, and wonders at the bad taste of the public who admire his plays. He, therefore, scarcely deigns to notice his remark. But the idea finds favour, and the ladies request a sermon, the subject to be chosen, as on the previous evening, by chance. The Duc d'Enghien is also urgent for a sermon, and M. de Montausier supports Madame de Longueville's and Julie's authoritative "Monsieur l'Abbé *must* preach us a sermon." Madame de Rambouillet seems rather to object to this new amusement of the *salon bleu*, but preparations are made, as before. The company seat themselves; the much mortified *abbé* steps on the daïs. The text is handed to him, and a general inclination to laugh aloud seizes this irreverent assembly when the *abbé* reads, "I said in my haste, All men are liars;" for all apply the text to the *abbé* himself, who has contended with and contradicted every one who spoke in favour of the student preacher.

The Abbé Cotin had preached too many sermons, bad or indifferent though they may have been, to be entirely at fault. The text is not one he would have selected to preach upon at all, much less without previous preparation. He gets through an exordium of some sort, and the "Ave Maria" is said. But here his eloquence comes to an end. He proceeds with a few disjointed phrases, but it is evident he finds nothing more to say. His lady friends perceive his embarrassment. Some are wicked enough to enjoy it; but one, who takes an especial interest in him, is resolved to save him. She utters a scream. There is general confusion. What is the matter with the lady? "Heavens! a spider, or something, has run over her dress, and she is always so nervous." The sermon is forgotten; all rush to the lady's assistance, and she is carried to a sofa, lamenting that she should have interrupted the strain of eloquence with which M. l'Abbé was about to edify the company. He proposes to return to the daïs, but his fair congregation is disposed to be merciful to its old-established favourite. The nerves of some are unstrung, they declare, by the fright just received; others think it too late to resume the discourse. M. de Montausier says to his friends, "*Soyons généreux*," and the *grands seigneurs* decamp in a body. The *abbé*, seeing his congregation melting away, protests that he is unfairly used. "*À demain, à demain, donc!*" he exclaims. But the Marquise de Rambouillet steps in and puts a decided *veto* on all attempts again to preach sermons in the *salon bleu*.

CHAPTER XXI.

Old Paris. — A Leader of Fashion. — Reappears on the Cours. — Mdlle. Ninon de Lenclos. — Returns to the World. — Grief for the Loss of her Mother. — Representative Women. — Ninon's Accomplishments. — Soon Weary of Rambouillet. — The Salon of Ninon. — Theories of the Abbé Gedouyn. — The Court of the Marais. — The Queen's Order to Ninon. — A Pavilion at the Grands Chartreux. — A Lady of very high Merit. — Ninon strives to make a Convert.

OLD PARIS, in spite of its walls, its bastions, and ditches, its crooked lanes, gutters, and rubbish-heaps, was a far pleasanter city in 1645 than it was twenty-five years before. It had at least one long, lively street, in the *beau quartier*, the Rue St. Antoine, in which were its best and gayest shops, as well as some of its finest hôtels. Then there were the Botanic and the Tuileries Gardens, the Cours de la Reine, and the gardens of the Place Royale, all completed and improved. The people also were in some degree less rough-mannered. They were certainly lighter in spirit and were looking forward to peace and its results: increase of commerce and increase of wealth. There was some improvement, too, in the form and size of the carriages of the wealthy, and their number was greater. The *calèche*, in which the ladies now took an airing on the Cours, or from the Porte Saint Bernard to Vincennes, was a less cumbrous vehicle than had hitherto been in use, and with its four horses, elaborately painted armorial bearings and showy liveries of the servants, made a dashing appearance.

One of the best-appointed and most elegantly adorned of those still rather capacious velvet-lined and fringed *calèches* might have been seen amongst the fashionable throng on the Cours on most of the fine days of the season. Its occupant was a lady with a fair share of beauty, elegantly dressed, young, and of graceful figure; she wore embroidered Spanish gloves, and carried her mask in her hand — less careful apparently of her fine clear complexion than were many ladies less fair than herself. She had fine dark eyes, a beautiful mouth, and when she smiled on any of the *beaux cavaliers* who saluted her with so much eagerness and seemed to vie with each for the honour or favour of a glance of recognition, you perceived that she had beautiful teeth, a personal attraction which not every *belle* of that day possessed. The Rambouillet family, with whom is Mademoiselle de Scudéry, just returned from Marseilles (Georges, who is "Gouverneur of the Fort de Notre Dame de la Garde," not being able longer to endure an exile from Paris), salute this fair lady, and Mesdames de Schomburg, De Chévreuse, and other *grandes dames* of the court, also exchange smiles and bows with her.

One haughty-looking *grand seigneur*, young, but evidently a person of great consideration from the attention he attracts, orders his carriage to be stopped, and alights to salute the fair lady of the *calèche*. He is known to be rather sparing in his attentions to the fair sex. He disdains to play, in this age of gallantry, the "*honnête et galant homme*" to any of the *belles* of the day. He has loved devotedly, passionately, a very beautiful and amiable girl, and desired to marry her. His family would not hear of it; it was deemed *une mésalliance*, and there was besides a *mariage de convenance*, which political reasons also made very desirable, then being adjusted between his friends and those of the lady. This marriage took place. The forsaken fair one retired to a convent to hide her grief under the black veil of a nun. Her lover became moody, and his temper was soured by disappointment. He sought to forget his sorrow in the profession of arms, and the fortune of war crowned him with glory, but without greatly blunting his regret for his lost first love. This distinguished youth was the hero of the hour, Louis de Bourbon, Duc d'Enghien, and the lady he has alighted from his carriage to salute is the celebrated Mademoiselle Ninon de Lenclos.

He wants to ask Ninon the question which the

whole of the fashionable world has been asking of late,—"where Mademoiselle Ninon has been hiding herself." She had disappeared from the Marais; her house in the Rue des Tournelles had been closed, and all visitors received from the persons in charge the same reply, "Mademoiselle Ninon was away, and it was not known when she would return." It was whispered about that she had retired to the convent of the Carmelites, previous to taking the veil. Few gave credence to this report; those who believed they well understood her character, shook their heads and smiled.

"It was contrary to Ninon's known principles," they said,—"principles founded on the philosophy of Montaigne, of whom, and his imitator, Charon, she was a constant and an ardent student."

Her devoted and life-long friend, Saint Évremond, when questioned, replied gravely, "that a family affliction, which had deeply affected Mademoiselle de Lenclos, had induced her to seclude herself for a time."

The reappearance of Ninon's *calèche* on the Cours caused as great a sensation as would that of some leader of fashion in "the drive" or "the row," after being mysteriously missing for a whole season. It was remarked, too, as in some sort confirming Saint Évremond's account, that, although dressed with her usual elegance, Mademoiselle Ninon was in mourning — deep mourning — rich black brocade, with narrow puffings of violet satin, and ruffles and *fichu* of fine point lace. Her gloves were black, embroidered in violet and gold, with gold fringes at the top, and attached by gold tassels. She was enveloped in a kind of hood or mantilla of fine black taffetas, fringed with gold and embroidered. A long string of pearls completed her *toilette;* and it was generally agreed that Ninon had never looked more *distinguée*, or more charming, though she was a little paler than usual.

She had not abstained in her mourning from the use of rouge, which in those high-rouging days was frequently the mode in which fashionable grief was displayed, for Ninon never wore rouge. Anne of Austria had rouged to excess until the death of Louis XIII., but had then discarded its use altogether. Many ladies were endeavouring, as was their duty, to follow her example; but having dyed their skins yellow by long use of paint, they now needed it to hide in some measure the defects it had caused. The bloom had temporarily faded from Ninon's cheek from excessive grief for the death of her mother, to whom she was devotedly attached. But severe and extreme piety* had led Madame de Lenclos to separate herself from her daughter in order to spend the evening of her life in the austere practices of religion.

Ninon mourned her loss deeply, and some feeling of self-reproach led her to retire to a convent

* "Vie de Ninon de Lenclos." A de Brot.

in the Faubourg Saint Honoré, with the intention of giving up the world. She declined to receive any of her friends, and only after repeated entreaties and refusals, Saint Évremond obtained permission to see her. He strove then to wean her from her purpose of adopting a course he believed she would repent of when the first anguish of grief had subsided; and at length prevailed on her to return to the world, which he felt persuaded was not yet altogether odious to her.

Ninon de Lenclos, who, like Madeleine de Scudéry, lived through the greater part of the seventeenth century, represents, also like her, a phase of its society. Madame de Rambouillet, la Duchesse de Longueville, la Marquise de Sablé, each in her sphere represents another, and each with a prevailing influence that led to the social supremacy of woman in France. Ninon was not of obscure birth; her father was a man of fair property, and of some culture. His philosophical views he instilled into the mind of his daughter. Plato was his oracle, and, together with Montaigne, became hers. Her mother, as a devotee, loved seclusion, but her father, well received himself, was able to introduce Ninon into the best society of the Marais and to the Rambouillet circle. She was an only child, and the property she derived from her family, and which she came into possession of at an early age, she managed with great ability and judgment. It enabled her to purchase a good house in the Rue des Tournelles (then one of the most frequented in Paris), and to live in comfort and ease — almost in affluence.

Her education was far superior to that of most women of the time. Her mother would have had her brought up and taught in a convent; her father considered that ignorant nuns must be incompetent teachers, therefore gave her for instructors the best professors he could obtain. She acquired Spanish and Italian, which then threatened to displace French at the court, and was acquainted with the works of the best writers in those languages, as well as in French. In dancing, the great accomplishment of the day, she excelled, and she sang pleasingly to the accompaniment of her lute. Introduced at Rambouillet at about the age of seventeen (she was born in 1616), her acquirements, her liveliness, her bright, sunny temper, her ingenuous and amiable character, even more than her beauty, secured her at once many friends.

She may have acquired there the "art of conversing well;" for we are told of the brilliancy of her conversational powers as well as of her exquisite manners and enchanting smile, her tact, and penetration into character. Her admiring biographer, M. de Brot, sums up her perfections in the words, "*Femme inimitable en tout, et que sous le règne merveilleux de Louis XIV. fixa les yeux des adorateurs du mérite distingué.*" Acting, however, on the principles of her favourite, Montaigne, who loved ease and independence, and was an enemy to all constraint, she soon wearied of Rambouillet. She liked its refinements, its elegant surroundings and amusements; but characterized its learned discussions as *érudition sèche et stérile;* and the sentimental servitude and chivalric gallantry exacted by the ladies of the *salon bleu* from their "*amants inoffensifs*" or humble servants, "*les honnêtes et galants hommes,*" she termed "*affectations métaphysiques.*"

The notions of the advanced ladies of the nineteenth century are in some respects those professed by Ninon de Lenclos in the seventeenth. "*Je vois,*" she said, "*que les hommes nous ont chargé de ce qu'il a de plus frivole, et qu'ils se sont réservé le droit aux qualités essentielles. C'est une injustice; de ce moment je me fais homme.*" Thus emancipated, she opened a *salon* of her own. Unmeaning compliments, affected sentimentality, and long, pompous dissertations on Greek and Roman history, were prohibited there. A tone of good breeding was to prevail at her receptions; any breach of the manners of polite society excluded the offender. Conversation and music, the recitation of poems, the reading of new works, were to form the evening's amusement, and wit, genius and talent were peculiarly welcome to her. Her aim was to create a Rambouillet on a smaller scale, and to free it from the restraints imposed by etiquette which she considered excessive and a barrier to enjoyment.

Very soon no receptions were more numerously and brilliantly attended than Mademoiselle Ninon's. Her natural grace and elegance, her unaffected charm of manner, her winning smile and gentle voice, were too often, perhaps, fatally captivating, but never failed immediately to interest in her favour all who obtained an introduction to her. Every writer of her day speaks of her in terms of admiration,— not of her beauty only, but of the qualities of her mind — her wit, her vivacity, her intellect, her amiability, sincerity in friendship, and kindness of heart.

The Abbé Gedouyn, the translator of Quintilian and Pausanius, and the author of some severe strictures on Milton's "Paradise Lost," owed to Ninon's encouragement of the talent she discerned in him the reputation he acquired in his day. Gedouyn was *chanoine* of the Sainte Chapelle, and greatly devoted to the study of the writers of antiquity. Ninon entered into this study with very great interest; for Gedouyn traced in the mythological fables of Paganism emblems of the operations of a Divine power and an admirable system of natural philosophy. These speculations fascinated the mind of Ninon; she was prone to take up theories of this nature, and, later on in her life, to reason and philosophize upon them. "*Il fallait l'entendre dogmatiser,*" says Madame de Sévigné. "*C'était une philosophe,*" says another writer, "*mais une philosophe très aimable.*"

Whatever were the errors of Ninon, she was certainly a remarkable woman, and a very distinguished one in her day. The opulent society of the Marais, the rank and fashion of the court, the most celebrated of the *beaux esprits, littérateurs,* poets, marshals of France, dignitaries of the Church, etc., met in her *salons.* Women of the highest rank formed part of her circle, and were on intimate terms with her. And why not? On the score of morals, the court of "*la belle dame du Marais*" could well bear comparison with the court of Anne of Austria; while, in point of attractiveness, the intellectual conversation and *spirituel passe-temps* of the society of the former were far above comparison with the dreary, idle gossip that formed the chief delight of the ignorant and indolent queen-regent, and wearied the circle that assembled at the Palais Royal.

No wonder that the sudden disappearance of such a luminary from its orbit should have caused a sensation in the world of fashion, or that its shining forth again in full splendour should have been hailed with intensest satisfaction. But Ninon did not immediately after leaving the convent re-open her "painted saloon;" her loss was too recent, her grief still too poignant. When she did so, an anecdote relates (anecdotes should always be received with suspicion) that the increase in her circle was so great, owing to the numerous new introductions — or, as they should perhaps be termed, presentations, for there was some ceremoniousness observed on such occasions — that much jealousy was felt in rival *salons*, where there was, in consequence, a great falling off in the attendance. It was resolved to mention the circumstance to the queen. "*Cette Ninon*," she was told, "had, by her seductive arts, attracted to her house all the *grands seigneurs* of the court, and the most desirable *partis* in the kingdom."

The queen-regent was shocked — nay, alarmed — to hear of the arts of "the bewitching philosopher of the Marais;" for to her philosophy meant *diablerie*, and her piety at once took fright. Immediately she despatched an officer of the guard with an order to Ninon to retire to a convent. She suggested that of "*Les filles repenties*," but conceded to her the liberty of selection. The queen's messenger was very graciously received by the culprit, who was surprised while dining with her friends, Saint Évremond, Rochefoucauld (then Prince de Marsillac), the young Huguenot Count de Coligny, Mdme. de la Sablière, and Mdlle. de Scudéry. She read the queen's order to her guests. The gentlemen were indignant; the ladies astonished and terrified. But Ninon, treating the order as a jest, said "she was duly sensible of the honour conferred on her, and that she had no hesitation in selecting for her retreat one of the pavilions and gardens of the monastery of the 'Grands Chartreux,'* if her choice met with approval."

The officer, presuming on the general affability, and not infrequent undignified familiarity of the queen, ventured to repeat, with a smile, Mademoiselle Ninon's exact reply. But Anne was horrified, and exclaimed angrily, "*Le monastère des Grands Chartreux! mais, la vilaine!*"

The captain of *les gardes*, M. de Gentaut, who was a friend of Ninon, perceiving that the queen was really displeased, stepped forward and assured her that "Mademoiselle de Lenclos's answer could have been no message intended for her majesty. It was mere *badinage*, in reply to an order she probably had treated as a joke, as she was a lady held in great consideration, and deservedly so, from her many attractions and estimable qualities."

The testimony of M. de Gentaut was confirmed by M. de Voiture and other gentlemen who were present, and a few of the ladies. The queen, who had begun to fear that she would be troubled to take further steps in the matter, lent a gracious and

---

* This monastery occupied an immense extent of ground. Its founder was Saint Louis. Each monk had a separate pavilion, which, with the numerous outbuildings of the monastery, the extensive gardens, and spacious church, formed almost a small town. The space is now covered with houses and streets.

willing ear to the praises of Ninon, complaining only of having been importuned by the *criailleries* of the envious to offer an affront to a lady of such very high merit — a lady possessing the esteem of "*les plus grands seigneurs de la cour*," and even honoured with the friendship of the severely virtuous Duc d'Enghien, the cynical Prince de Marsillac (then in great favour with Anne), and, above all, by that of M. de Voiture and the learned ladies of the "*société polie de l'Hôtel de Rambouillet.*" And so Ninon received no further order to "go to a nunnery — go." "*Le moyen*," says Madame de Sévigné, on another and later occasion, "*de n'être pas flattée de l'estime de M. le Prince, d'autant plus qu'il ne la jette pas à la tête des dames.*"

Another circumstance also told greatly with the queen in favour of Ninon. It was known that she had long set her heart on converting her Huguenot lover, De Coligny. Anne of Austria of course attributed this to religious zeal; but, unfortunately, Ninon would have been satisfied with his formal abjuration of Protestantism, without any real renunciation of faith in its doctrines. Coligny was ambitious, and that opportunities of distinguishing himself might more readily be afforded him, she employed all her powers of persuasion to draw him into the flock of "the faithful." She did not prevail, perhaps because she argued in favour of disingenuousness and against her own principles; for, according to her guiding system of philosophy, she professed to hold falsehood and deceit in abhorrence. She, however, gained with the queen some additional credit — which probably she would have been unwilling herself to accept — for her attempt to convert Coligny, whom her majesty pitied for his blindness and obstinacy.

CHAPTER XXII.

The Convent of Val Profond. — The Abbey of Val de Grace. — Mansard's Original Design. — Education of the Young Princes. — Lamothe Le Vayer. — A Princely Education. — Two Terrible Turks. — The Duties of Piety. — The Royal Brothers. — The Court at Fontainebleau. — The Swedish Ambassador. — The Daughter of the "Ice-King." — Cartesian Philosophy. — The Ambassador Perplexed. — His Troubled Spirit Soothed.

SOON after Anne of Austria had abandoned the Louvre, and made the Palais Royal her residence, she set about the accomplishment of her vow to found a religious house as a thank-offering to God for the birth of a son. She had already established, in the Faubourg Saint Jacques, the Benedictine nuns of the convent of Val Profond; but as the sympathy of Louis XIII. was not with her in her project, its full realization was necessarily deferred. The original plans for the magnificent church and abbey of Val de Grace were prepared by François Mansard, under whose superintendence the building was begun. Louis XIV. laid the first stone of the church. He was seven years old when this, his first public act, was performed. Some cabal against Mansard caused him to discontinue the work; alterations were introduced into his designs, and four other architects completed the edifice. The whole of the elaborate decorations had reference to the birth of Christ, and were intended to convey allusions to that of Louis XIV. The fresco paintings of the cupola were by Mignard. They contain two hundred figures, representing the various orders of saints adoring the Trinity, and, in the midst, the queen and Saint Louis offering to the Deity the model of the church of Val de Grace.

The paintings of the communion chapel were by Philippe de Champaigne. The magnificent sculptures of the dome were by Michel Anguier, an artist of great talent. The French excelled in sculpture, as the beautiful work of the sixteenth and seventeenth centuries in the Louvre attests, and that still existing in churches, in the few remaining hôtels of the *noblesse*, and even here and there in some house of less pretensions, which has hitherto wholly, or in part, escaped destruction. The celebrated group of "La Crèche," now in the church of Saint Roch, belonged to the church of Val de Grace; it stood under the baldachin, and was considered the *chef-d'œuvre* of the sculptor, François Anguier. This beautiful church was used as a warehouse from the time of the revolution until 1826; the abbey was transformed into a military hospital. François Mansard, its first architect, on being deprived of the superintendence of the building of the edifice, erected for M. de Guénégaud, at his Château de Fresne, a small chapel, a *bijou* of its kind, representing, in miniature, the original design of the church of Val de Grace.

But while Anne of Austria's sumptuous thank-offering to God was rapidly advancing towards completion, the child whose birth had called forth this pious gratitude was growing up neglected and ignorant. Education of some kind was needful for the king and his brother, and this caused her very great embarrassment. While infants, she had expressed an intention of having them "instructed in every science;" a few years later she was in doubt whether the sciences were an appropriate study for princes, and was inclined to think Latin more worthy the attention of youthful royalty. History, or geography, she had no idea of herself; it therefore never occurred to her that it was needful to burden the brain, or weary attention by acquiring the knowledge of any history except the historiettes and intrigues of the court. She believed that Mazarin was, of all men in Europe, the most able, the most learned, and the most *spirituel;* therefore, the most competent to decide on the course of study best adapted for her sons. To his tender mercies, therefore, she left them.

Mazarin chose first, for the post of governor

to the young king, the Marquis de Villeroi. He had held high command in the army, was supposed to be well acquainted with the interior condition of the kingdom — knowledge then possessed but by few — and to have some ability as a statesman. Villeroi desired the rank of Maréchal de France, and received it, together with his appointment of governor. It was not, however, for his merits that it was conferred, but to ensure his acquiescence in the views of Mazarin. For preceptor, he selected Beaumont de Péréfixe, Archbishop of Paris, and the author of the most attractively written life extant of Henry IV. It was intended for the edification of his pupil, and is a pleasing but fanciful portrait of the dissolute monarch, the roistering *vaurien*, whose failings, if, according to the archbishop, he had any, were but "*les faiblesses d'un homme aimable.*"

As the duties of M. de Péréfixe were almost nominal, the young king received for the first year such casual instruction as M. Lamothe le Vayer, who had been named preceptor to Philippe, the king's brother, had inclination or time to impart to him. Le Vayer was a man of much talent, engaged in abstruse literary and scientific studies. Among the learned he gained some reputation by his work on "La vertu des Païens," in which he strove to confute the idea, then prevalent, that the morality of the modern, or Christian world, was of a higher tone than that which predominated amongst the pagan nations of antiquity—a task of no great difficulty then, or even in this virtuous age, one would imagine.

Le Vayer soon discovered that Louis was far less intelligent than his younger brother Philippe, and, on the education of the former being transferred to the charge of another preceptor, was disposed really to interest himself in developing the talent he believed he had discerned in his youthful pupil. But the watchful eye of Mazarin was upon him. The *rusé* cardinal's design was that both brothers should receive "a princely education." That of the one destined to ascend the throne was to be "monarchical and Catholic;" which meant that, before all things, it was to be constantly impressed upon him that he was a king, therefore "a being essentially superior to other men." "*Qu'il doit avoir pour but la glorie et pour moyen la force; que la nation réside toute entière dans la personne du monarque; que les sujets doivent obéir sans contrôler les décrets du roi,*" etc.

"What could you be thinking of," said Mazarin to Le Vayer, "when you proposed to make a clever man of the king's brother? If he had more learning than the king, would he not be able often to put him to the blush, and would he then be disposed to obey him?"

Such are the base and narrow views attributed to Mazarin, and the conduct of the king and his brother in manhood was the natural result of such a system. Villeroi, when he became thoroughly initiated into Mazarin's views, expressed much regret that he had not sooner been aware of them, and is said to have endeavoured, in some measure, to counteract them by engaging the young king in conversation, and in that way interesting him in things it was desirable he should be instructed in. The princes were not even taught to read until they had become so thoroughly idle and indisposed for study that there was no longer any fear of their using such knowledge to acquire information for themselves. They were left entirely to the charge of sub-tutors, who, to every remark on the backwardness or idleness of these children, were always able to reply that "the Superior," Mazarin, "reserved to himself the right of regulating the course of studies to be pursued by their royal pupils." A translation of Cæsar's "Commentaries," and another of Florus, were published in the names of the king and Philippe d'Orléans, though neither of them understood a word of Latin, nor scarcely could write his own name. Both, then, read French with difficulty, and orthography was never mastered by Louis XIV.

They both acquired the worst habits, from

associating with the lowest servants of the household—pilfering, scratching, fighting, lying, and using gross language, Philippe being by no means an obedient subject, in his youth, to his high and mighty brother. The education of *un grand seigneur* was then comprised in dancing, riding, and fencing. If he knew anything more, he owed it generally to a natural bent for the acquirement of knowledge, rather than to facilities afforded him for obtaining it. Learning was for the *canaille*, as "*la grande reine*" was pleased to call the lawyers, the magistrates, and others to whom a course of study at the university or colleges was necessary. Hence the contempt so long felt by the empty-headed grandees for men of letters, and which the Marquise de Rambouillet helped to abolish.

Anne of Austria was fond of her children, and proud of their aptitude in acquiring the accomplishments befitting *les beaux cavaliers*, for they could ride and dance already, and were anxious to have the foils in their hands. Louis was her favourite, as the inheritor of the "right divine." She herself instructed him in the duties of piety, showed him her collection of reliques, explained whence they came, their value in the sight of Heaven, and the benefits innumerable they brought down on their possessor; knowledge which she believed to be of far greater importance to him than any that a preceptor or tutor could impart. He learned very early the etiquette of the court, the profound homage due to his own sacred little person, and was initiated betimes into the ceremonies of "the public toilette," by being invested with the privilege of presenting the queen's chemise. When he left the royal presence he joined his brother, even more neglected than himself, and together they made a raid on the cupboards and store-rooms, and stole cakes, sweets, etc., which they ate in secret, observing, doubtless, no etiquette or ceremony whatever while enjoying the fruits of their joint petty larceny. Thus these young princes grew up like plants running to seed, without care or culture, for no moral restraints were imposed on them, no moral principles inculcated; but, on the contrary, every effort was made by the myrmidons of Mazarin to destroy any germ of good that might appear in them, and to implant evil in its stead.

The queen-regent's infatuation for Mazarin cost her the good opinion of the people, and her excessive anxiety to make him popular had but the effect of intensifying the ill-feeling with which they already regarded him. There were signs of France being ill at ease under the rule of one who was often called "*le serpent qui avait succédé au tigre;*" there were indications in another country of a people being roused to rebellion by tyranny, and a threatening of revolt against the oppression of rulers becoming epidemic in Europe. This was displeasing to Anne; it occasioned anxiety, disturbed the even tenour of her life. All had gone smoothly since her accession to power; life had glided on, day succeeded day in a delightfully pleasant if somewhat monotonous round. She resolved to change the scene, and to seek undisturbed quiet at Fontainebleau.

The principal change in the daily programme was that the queen and the ladies and gentlemen of her court and household, after promenading in the sand and dust of the forest, spent a few hours in the shallow part of the Seine. The princes and their governor were of the party — "*La modestie*," says Madame de Motteville, "*n'y était nullement blessée*"— for both ladies and gentlemen wore grey linen chemises reaching to the ground. They chatted and promenaded, the conversation being "*gaie et libre*," while the more lively of the party danced and sang.

The Comte de la Gardie, the ambassador of Queen Christina, followed or accompanied the court to Fontainebleau. He appears to have taken with him a new state carriage which Christina had ordered from the king's coachbuilder in Paris; and while the bathers were engaged in their frolics in the water, M. de la Gardie favoured them with a *grand spectacle* on the banks of the river. The Swedish queen's coach, in all the splendour of new velvet, gold and silver fringes and embroidery, and drawn by six richly caparisoned horses, attended by twelve pages in black and yellow silver-laced liveries, went trotting up and down, followed by the ambassador himself, in an equipage scarcely less splendid than that of his royal mistress. Two portly coachmen, to match the size of the carriages, as well as numerous attendants on foot, in the orange and silver liveries of the court, completed this effective and splendid "turn out." It gave the spectators a high idea of the grandeur and state of Christina of Sweden.

Christina, then in her twentieth year, was celebrated throughout Europe for her learning; all the heroic virtues of the illustrious women of antiquity were also attributed to her, so that her ambassador was readily believed when he proceeded to descant on her extraordinary attainments and virtues, as surpassing all that renown had spread abroad concerning them. De la Gardie was himself a personage of unusually lofty pretensions. Christina, in opposition to the advice and entreaties of Oxenstierna, had put the country to an inconvenient and unnecessary expense in sending a splendid embassy to France, and, at the head of it, with princely appointments, this favourite, whom alone she thought worthy of representing a royal mistress so distinguished.

"Instead of making men die of love for her, as she might have done," so the count told the queen-regent and her ladies, "she made them ready to hang themselves with shame and disgust when, bowing before the might of her masculine intellect, they were compelled to confess what poor weak creatures, in comparison with her, they were." This account of the daughter of the "great Ice-king" was received by the fair dames the ambassador addressed with profound awe and respect. He told them, further, that the Swedish queen had fully considered Descartes's system of philosophy and could not give it her approval.

This astonished the queen-regent; she expressed much surprise and even some regret to hear it. She, however, knew nothing of Descartes or his system; his philosophy was not the rage of the *salons* until several years later, and at the time referred to only some especially philosophical *bleue belle* of the Rambouillet circle could have been interested in it or professed herself a Cartesienne. But Anne had heard of another celebrated lady to whom had been applied the term "learned and *amiable* philosopher" — a lady who, while willingly receiving homage to her intellect, did not forbid lovers to die for her. The most distinguished of the *grands seigneurs* and *grandes dames* of the court had but lately sung in chorus the praises of this "*amiable* philosopher," and — as the queen remembered with satisfaction — prevented some indignity from being offered to her.

Now Anne of Austria felt no sympathy whatever with the *severity* which the Swedish ambassador attributed to his queen as a merit; and on learning further that there was a system of philosophy to which Christina took objection, she very naturally thought she discovered in that the cause of her hardness of heart, and that, therefore, it was much to be lamented. De la Gardie, not comprehending the queen's allusions, began to explain the views of Descartes, in order to justify Christina — his argument being as intelligible to the queen as a discourse in Hebrew or Greek. If etiquette had permitted, both she and her ladies would have yawned outright, so frightfully did he weary them. And what really would have been the consequence, Heaven only knows — for the young count was mercilessly in earnest, and denounced with much energy Descartes's limited range of ideas, his too exclusive spirit, his intolerance of discussion, his precipitation and presumption, his extremely vague and abstract principles, and so forth — had not Anne raised her eyes to the timepiece that crowned the high Venetian cabinet before which De la Gardie was standing. The queen perceived that the hour for retiring to her oratory had arrived, and no amusements, or even the most important affairs of state—could her presence have had any influence on them — were allowed to interfere with her stated times for devotion. She rose, — De la Gardie understood the signal. In her usual affable manner, she thanked him for the "amusement he had afforded her," adding, with a smile, that he had "quite convinced her that philosophy was, after all that could be said in its favour, but a dreary thing indeed."

The young ambassador bowed low, very low, to hide a certain confusion of face, and as Anne, followed by her ladies, passed to her oratory, he slowly withdrew, — perplexed and annoyed at the sarcastic tone, as he conceived, of the queen's remarks. The more his thoughts dwelt on the subject, the more he was troubled in spirit. He felt that either his own or his royal mistress's superlative merit was not duly appreciated at the French court, and that it would be well to request his recall. He was mistaken, at least so far as Christina was concerned, — she had to appear in person to dispel the *prestige* her name had acquired in France, and to prove how uncertain, how little to be relied upon, are the sounds given forth by the trumpet of renown.

Christina had written a letter to the queen-regent in French, another to the cardinal minister, and a third to Monsieur le Duc d'Orléans. The sentiments she expressed towards France had given great satisfaction, and her facility in the use of a foreign tongue had been the subject of much encomium and compliment. De la Gardie's equanimity was restored, and he reported to his sovereign the high esteem with which her exalted character and marvellous abilities were regarded at the French court. *Fêtes*, balls, and banquets had been given in her honour. One thing, however, he was fain to confess, — the queen-regent held opinions which appeared to him to be very erroneous on the subject of the Cartesian philosophy.

CHAPTER XXIII.

Musical Art in its Infancy. — The Band of Les Mousquetaires. — A Promenade Concert. — Celebrities of the Court. — De la Rochefoucauld. — The French Navy. — Les Beaux Mousquetaires. — Le Comte de Coligny.

AT the period we are writing of, music as an art was in its infancy in France. The voice of Angélique Paulet may have had fatal effects on envious nightingales; it may have filled other listeners with wonder and delight, as its thrilling tones lent beauty to some simple French or Spanish air, supported, or rather accompanied, by the tinkling of the graceful and pretty, but feeble lute, — for this was the highest effort of musical art then attained in the *salons*, and to have accomplished so much was to enjoy, as she did, social reputation as a musician. The théorbe was merely a lute of larger size, and was sometimes used with the violins, which were greatly in request, to play lively airs to give animation to the *ballets* then in vogue, and in which there was as much acting as dancing. Lulli was still in his native Florence, whence, soon after, at the age of thirteen or fourteen, he was brought to France by the Chevalier de Guise, whom Mademoiselle de Montpensier had asked to find her an Italian page.

Military music one can scarcely imagine to have been very inspiriting. "The music of a march," it is probable, shed little, if any, "joy on duty." We indeed hear of the Duc d'Enghien, when about to besiege Lerida, opening the trenches to the accompaniment of a band of violins, and we are at once transported, in fancy, to the bloodless scene of some operatic combat, rather than to the scene of war's alarms and the din of real battle. But who has not heard of *"les beaux mousquetaires"* — *" mousquetaires noirs ; mousquetaires gris ; mousquetaires de la reine"* ? These "crack corps" were chiefly composed of very fine gentlemen, but, as a rule, *un peu mauvais sujets*. They were as exclusive as the famous 10th — "they didn't dance." But they had a band of cymbals and trumpets. There is a sort of roughness and clang to the delicate ear even in the name of those instruments, and a band of such music would seem to be more likely to excite, than to "soothe the savage breast." Yet the gallant mousquetaires not unfrequently sent their band to the gardens of La Place Royale, to give pleasure to the many bright stars of fashion and beauty who resided in that favourite *locale*. And in skilful hands the sounds produced by cymbals and trumpets may be so modulated as to produce a pleasing effect.

At all events, they pleased the fair dames of

that day, and whenever these concerts took place the gardens were thronged. What a pretty and picturesque scene to look down upon from one of the broad balconies of the *Place!* What a display of feathers and lace, long strings of unwrought pearls and silken stuffs! what a variety of colours, bright as the flowers in the *parterres!* How graceful the hoods and hongrelines, and what elaborate *coiffures!* All those frizzings and curlings, *rouleaux*, ribands, and lappets must need much time and skill to erect and rightly arrange. But time was of small account then. Dressing and gambling, and being adored comprised the whole duty of woman, and there was plenty of time for that. The dresses are really superb. "*Les dames de qualité*," says Sauval, "spend more in gloves and fans and trimmings, and such like *galanteries*, than foreign princesses expend on themselves and their whole household."

All the celebrities of the court might be seen promenading in the Place Royale when the mousquetaire cymbals and trumpets performed. There is Madame la Princesse, more haughty than ever, and the hero of Rocroi at her side; there the beautiful Madame de Longueville, with the Comte de Coligny — Ninon's *cher ami* — in assiduous attendance upon her. This excites much notice and comment, and many significant glances are exchanged amongst the ladies.

There, sauntering together, are the Duchesse de Montbazon and her humble servant, the Duc de Longueville; the Marquise de Sablé, too, and her friend De la Rochefoucauld. She is building a house for herself within the precincts of Port Royal; by no means to retire from the world, but to enjoy society or to devote herself to religion, just as she may feel inclined. She has many habits and traits of character in common with the queen; she is desperately idle, has an excellent appetite, and is fond of pampering it, and, like Anne of Austria, thinks that *"la belle galanterie"* and devotion should walk hand-in-hand; but she has had more education than the queen, and is fond of literary society. She is distinguished for "*les belles manières*," and is especially prone to construct "*maximes et pensées.*"

La Rochefoucauld looks as if he were not well pleased; he has a surly air. Saint Simon has told us that a morose, proud temper was a characteristic of his family. Just now he may be excused, for he has reason to be displeased with the queen, towards whom both he and Beaufort-Vendôme were inclined to display much chivalric devotion. But the cardinal stepped in and prevented Anne from fulfilling the promises she had made of giving La Rochefoucauld the governorship of Normandy. She looked coldly on him, too; no longer bestowed

Duke de la Rochefoucauld

on him one of those smiles that Madame de Motteville tells us were so irresistible. La Rochefoucauld resented this treatment, and joined "*Les Importants*," the party opposed to Mazarin. Beaufort was the chief of this party. He had desired to be placed at the head of the admiralty. The cardinal refused to gratify him; he thought him incompetent, and disliked him for his popularity; generally, too, the duke was considered fit only to play the part of "*un héros de théâtre*." But as the entire French navy then consisted of but two or three rotten vessels, no great ability was needed to direct that department of the state. Beaufort was indignant, and became the cardinal's enemy.

But look once more at the company. There is Mademoiselle Ninon, and she is escorted by her friend Saint Évremond and a dashing *mousquetaire noir*. She wears a violet dress with a woven-in pattern of black and gold. France has begun to be famous for those thick rich silks. Several of these mousquetaires have ridden up to join the gay throng from their barracks, or hôtel, as it is called, on the road to Charenton, just beyond the Bastille. They leave their horses and their large riding-cloaks — which cover up their horses as well as themselves — with their servants, who wait their return outside on the *Place*. Nearly the whole of the *mousquetaire corps* are Gascons and cadets of good family; for in Gascony the younger sons have to seek their fortune in the world. They are a dashing set of men, rather boastful in Gascon fashion, fond of vaunting their prowess, and success in sunning themselves in the light of bright eyes and ladies' smiles; but they are overflowing with valour, are generally good-tempered, and bear a resemblance — more or less marked — to the popular Gascon king.

They wear black or gray short coats, a large cross on the breastplate, like the ancient Templars, felt hats with a flying plume, wide pantaloons, with high wrinkled leather boots and large brass spurs. They are extremely well lodged in a spacious hôtel with fine gardens and ample stabling. It has a fencing saloon, a riding-house, and a *cour d'honneur*. They are favourites — very great favourites — in this fashionable faubourg of the Marais; and it is not without reason they bear themselves with that jaunty air you may remark as they join the *beau monde* in the garden, and lift their plumed hats with that self-assured smile to the brightest belles, seeming to ask — with no doubt of the reply — "Are we not charming fellows?"

The trumpets and cymbals have come to the end of their programme, and the company begin to disperse. The princes D'Enghien and De

Conti have decamped with their mother and sister. Young De Coligny passes over to say a few words to Mademoiselle Ninon, who is not the least in the world displeased that he has transferred his attentions to the beautiful duchess, though she knows he has lately obtained leave to sigh at her feet "*en galant et honnête homme.*" He excuses himself for not joining her sooner, but with a gay yet somewhat derisive laugh, she "bids him go lie at the feet of his duchess, and sigh there, and die there, too, if he choose." Her *calèche* drives up; Saint Évremond and her mousquetaire friend hand her in. Coligny follows in the train of Madame de Montbazon, who lives in the Place Royale, and with whom many of the promenaders have returned to converse, play picquet, and amuse themselves during the rest of the afternoon. Poor Coligny! and he really has to die for his duchess. Alas! that the musical comedietta of the morning should result in a tragedy.

CHAPTER XXIV.

The Mysterious Billets-doux. — To Whom do they Belong? — Rival Belles. — A Tale of Turpitude. — The Lover and the Husband. — Public Apology Demanded. — Difficult Diplomacy. — A Doubtful Peace. — Dispersion of "Les Importants." — Coligny Challenges De Guise. — A Duel on the Place Royale. — Death of De Coligny. — "Argentan et Ismanie." — Triste Renown of the Duchess.

THE young Count de Coligny remained but a short time in the *salons* of the Duchesse de Montbazon. Soon after his departure, a lady of the company picked up two letters that were lying on the floor, and handed them to the duchess. They were without either signature or address, were written in a feminine hand, and proved to be love-letters, rather impassioned in style, for the duchess made no scruple of reading them for the general amusement of the guests. Curiosity was piqued. "Who could have written them?" "Who was the recipient?" "Had any of the company who entered with her left the Hôtel?" Several had left. "But the last to leave," exclaims the duchess with unconcealed delight, "was Maurice de Coligny." "Unawares he must have let them fall from his pocket," says another. "To whom *could* they belong but Maurice?" cry two or three voices in chorus. "They are his, I am certain; but who is the writer?" says Madame de Montbazon, malignantly, and almost in a whisper, as she casts her eyes searchingly round the *salon*. The Duc de Longueville happens to be absent, which is rather unusual, so persistently does he haunt the Hôtel de Montbazon.

The duchess, therefore, in a tone intended to suggest rather than to assert, says, "*La belle des belles?*" The sympathizing *grandes dames* smile significantly their assent,—a smile difficult indeed to describe, but one readily imagined by all women who have been present (and where is the woman who has not?) when an absent acquaintance, or friend, if you will, of whom a little jealousy was felt, has been maligned.

Madame de Montbazon had been jealous of the young Duchesse de Longueville from the time that her marriage was first announced with the duke, though he had made no effort to break from the chains in which she still held him. She believed that all the beauty of the court paled before her own; but to her secret horror she was verging on that period of life the French are pleased to stigmatize as the "*terrible quarantaine.*" Her possible rival was yet in her teens, and this was not a pleasant thought to her. When she heard that small-pox had attacked the beautiful bride, she looked anxiously for her reappearance in society, not doubting but that the name so generally given to her of "*la belle des belles*" could no longer be applied, except derisively. How, then, was she mortified when compelled to acknowledge that the dreaded scourge of beauty had swept over her rival's lovely face without leaving a trace or an impress discernible, even to her searching eyes. But her faithful *cicisbeo* continued unswervingly to dance attendance upon her, which might have been gratifying had not the young duchess — while showing utter indifference to it — maintained her "*grande réputation de vertu et de sagesse.*"

Madame de Montbazon was not of the Rambouillet circle, but she well understood the theory of the "*amour chevalresque,*"

"*En ciel un Dieu,
En terre une déesse,*"

and that "*les honnêtes et galants hommes*" were merely "*amants inoffensifs,*" illustrative of the idea, gaining increased prevalence in polite French society, that woman was a superior being, to whom the homage of respectful admiration was to be unceasingly offered. The letters that had fallen into her hands breathed a different spirit from that permitted to the high-flown chivalry in vogue. They were compromising to the writer, and the writer, it was boldly asserted in all the *salons* of the party "*des importants,*" was the Duchesse de Longueville. As the story travelled from *salon* to *salon* of the Place Royale to the court, it became a terrible tale of turpitude, all malignant suspicions and suggestions caught up on its course being added to it as ascertained facts.

When the letters were found, the real culprits, Madame de Fouquerelles and the *beau* Marquis de Maulemont, were present. The latter dared not claim them and acknowledge that he had just then carelessly dropped them. It would have compromised the lady, who was in a dreadful fright lest her handwriting should be recognized. The marquis, however, confided his secret to La Rochefoucauld, who had some influence with Madame de Montbazon. Having assured her that an *éclat* was imminent that would have unpleasant results for herself, as it could be proved beyond doubt that neither the duchess nor Coligny had aught to do with the letters, La Rochefoucauld begged her earnestly to place them in his hands. Alarmed on her own account, she entrusted them to him. They were then shown to the Prince and Princess de Condé and their sons; to the Duc de Longueville, Madame de Rambouillet, Madame de Sablé, and, last of all, to the queen, in whose presence, the innocence of the young duchess being fully recognized, the letters were burnt,—greatly to the relief of Madame de Fouquerelles and her lover, who had suffered agony of mind from fear of detection, and were well content to leave the innocent to bear the ignominy they had escaped.

The duke, desirous of sparing annoyance to his mistress at the expense of his wife's reputation, advised that no further steps should be taken in the matter. Madame la Princesse and her sons were not so leniently disposed. The reparation, they said, must be as public as the offence, and the family must withdraw from the court if the queen and her minister did not undertake to avenge their injured honour. "Were the feelings of the granddaughter of a cook to be put in comparison with the honour of a princess of the blood!" The "*importants*," however, headed by the Duke de Guise, endeavoured to dissuade the queen from yielding to the Condé party. The Duchesse de Chévreuse, step-daughter of Madame de Montbazon, supported the claim of the princess, reminding Anne of her services to her when her own honour was called in question. The queen hesitated; but Mazarin could not afford to make enemies of the hero of Rocroi and his family. His opinion was favourable to them, and was, of course, law to the queen.

The Duchesse de Longueville, when this unexpected storm broke over her, retired to a country house belonging to the family, at La Barre, a short distance from Paris, to hide from the world her grief and vexation. There the queen visited her, and consoled her with promises of protection and satisfaction for the insult she had received.

All the *finesse* of the cardinal, and the skill of that practised *intrigante*, the Duchesse de Chévreuse, were exerted to prepare satisfactorily the apology, and the harangue that was to form the reply. It taxed their powers to the utmost. Every word underwent a long discussion before they agreed to accept or reject it. No public act involving the fate of nations ever needed for its satisfactory adjustment more skilful diplomacy. And the cardinal at the same time was doing his utmost to induce the opposing parties to come to a private explanation and arrangement. In vain he employed his winning tongue to induce one side to acknowledge too much, the other to accept too little. Again he and Madame de Chévreuse, with as much assiduity as if their own welfare and the happiness of their lives depended upon it, applied themselves to the task of arranging a peace on terms that should gain the approval of their clients.

At last a form was produced. The queen insisted on its acceptance. Madame de Montbazon was to go to the Hôtel de Condé, and there, in the presence of the whole Condé family and their intimate friends, was to protest that " she had never for one moment given any credit to what had been said respecting the letters and their supposed writer. The virtuous life of the

Duchesse de Longueville was so well known to her, that she could only attribute the slander to *les méchants esprits.*" That she might omit no word of this short address, it was written, and, to refresh her memory if necessary, attached to her fan. She chose to read it, and in so haughty a manner, and with an expression so satirical, that the princess felt more offended than satisfied by it. She also omitted to address the princess as "Madame." The cardinal being present at this scene as witness on the part of the queen-regent, insisted, the princess having complained, that Madame de Montbazon should re-commence the address and go through it again; which accordingly was done, though with considerable reluctance on the part of the culprit.

Few could surpass the Princesse de Condé in haughtiness, and in her most crushing manner she replied: "Madame, I accept willingly your assurance that you have had no part whatever in those malicious reports lately circulated; deferring in this matter to the commands laid upon me by the queen." The princess also obtained the queen's permission to refrain from appearing at any place, on any occasion, when the Duchesse de Montbazon was present. But the duchess sought every opportunity of appearing publicly where she knew the princess was likely to be, and refused to leave the Jardin de Renaud when a private request that she would do so was sent to her by the queen. The consequence was a letter from the minister, signed by the young king, ordering Madame de Montbazon to quit Paris.

This was more than her lovers and friends and the partizans of "*les importants*" were disposed quietly to allow. They resented it as a disgrace due to the insinuations of Mazarin. A plot was organized to displace him. It was whispered into the ear of the queen. Roused to energy by the monstrous audacity of the rebels who menaced the cardinal, she ordered the arrest of their ringleader, the Duc de Beaufort, and his transfer from the Louvre to Vincennes. The Bishop of Beauvais, who had entered into their scheme, was invited to repair to his diocese, and the Ducs de Vendôme and Mercœur were ordered to their estates. Suspicion falling also on the Duchesse de Chévreuse, she was banished to Touraine, and Madame de Châteauneuf to Berri. Thus, the "*important*" party being scattered far and wide, and the Condé set triumphant, the troubles and civil dissensions that were so seriously to disturb the reign of Anne and her minister, were deferred for awhile.

But where all this time, it may be asked, was Maurice de Coligny, whose name had been associated in this scandal with that of the young Duchesse de Longueville? Poor Maurice had been ill. His father, too (Maréchal de Coligny, Duc de Châtillon), had been of opinion that he should hold aloof from this complicated scandal, lest he should further compromise the duchess. Restored to health, the young count disregarded the opinion of his family, and appeared on the scene to challenge somebody. One of the most devoted *serviteurs* of Madame de Montbazon was the Duc de Guise. He had warmly espoused her quarrel, but had refused to join Beaufort's plot against Mazarin. As the cardinal had always means of discovering the opponents of his power, as well as those who were neutrals (for of friends he can scarcely be said to have had any but the queen and the child-king), De Guise, though of the "*important*" party, had not been interfered with.

Neither the Duc d'Enghien nor Coligny could challenge De Beaufort, who was safely locked up at Vincennes; the former, therefore, allowed Coligny, as his name had been mixed up in the affair, to demand satisfaction from Madame de Montbazon's champion. De Guise accepted the challenge. Unfortunately, Coligny was an unskilful swordsman, De Guise an able and practised one. Duelling had long been strictly prohibited. Richelieu had issued an edict which decreed the punishment of death to the duellist who had mortally wounded his adversary, and he had rigorously enforced it. Yet the practice was continued, and with very slight abatement. Coligny was the great-grandson of Admiral Coligny, one of the first victims of the St. Bartholomew massacre, and the Duc de Guise the great-grandson of the Guise who, on that fatal day, was of the party that murdered the admiral.

Braving the edict, they selected the Place Royale for their meeting. When their seconds handed the swords to them, De Guise, addressing Coligny, said — alluding to the wars of the League — "*Nous allons venger les anciennes querelles de nos maisons, et on verra quelle différence il faut mettre entre le sang de Guise et celui de Coligny.*"

Coligny was soon disabled by his more skilful adversary, who, when he had thrown him to the ground, put his foot on his sword, and said, "*Je ne veux pas vous tuer, mais vous traiter comme vous méritez, pour vous êtes adressé à un prince de ma naissance, sans vous en avoir donné sujet.*" He then struck him with the flat of his sword-blade.

Roused by this indignity, the wounded man raised himself by a great effort, threw back his adversary, disengaged his sword, and the struggle was renewed. De Guise was wounded in the shoulder, but speedily overcame Coligny, who was deeply wounded in the sword-arm. Coligny was carried to the house of the Duc d'Enghien, and both combatants were cited to appear before the parliament for infringing the edict prohibiting duels. The Duc de Guise replied, haughtily, he should appear, but with a *cortége* of princes and *grands seigneurs*. The Duc d'Enghien announced that he should accompany his friend, the Count de Coligny. But poor De Coligny's wounds being unskilfully treated, amputation of the arm became necessary. Being too weak to support the suffering then attending such an operation, he died a few hours after it, full of grief and lamentation at having so unworthily defended the honour of his house and that of *la belle duchesse*.

The duchess is said to have witnessed the combat, concealed behind a curtain, from one of the windows of the Hôtel de Rohan, in the Place Royale. The Prince and Princesse de Condé blamed Coligny for provoking a duel he had not the ability to sustain, and the public voice generally was in favour of De Guise. The affair, from first to last, caused the greatest sensation throughout France. In Paris it was the engrossing subject of conversation with all classes of society; but the court and the *salons*, in discussing it, added many imaginary circumstances to the actual romantic facts and tragic ending of this dramatic episode of the court life of old Paris.

It furnished the subject of a romance that was prepared in great haste, and produced before general interest in the affair had begun to decline. It was entitled, "L'histoire d'Argentan et Ismanie." The demand, small as were its merits, exceeded even the expectation of the writer and publisher, and taxed the resources of the printer to supply it. While Coligny was yet living, the contemptuous jest was current in society that he had begged his life of his adversary, who, with a sneer and a kick, had granted it. Under the windows of the house where the duchess was supposed to be secluded, was sung the *chansonnette* that might have also been heard in every corner of Paris :—

> "*Essuyez vos beaux yeux,*
> *Madame de Longueville,*
> *Essuyez vos beaux yeux,*
> *Coligny se porte mieux.*
> *S'il a demandé la vie*
> *Ne l'en blamez nullement,*
> *Car c'est pour être votre amant*
> *Qu'il veut vivre éternellement.*"

The Coligny party had also their songs in dispraise of Guise, so that old feuds and dissensions were revived, and with something of the old bitterness, from the circumstance of the duellists being the descendants of the two most illustrious combatants of the wars of the League.

The sad event gave a kind of *triste* renown to the Duchesse de Longueville. Her name became popular amongst the lower as well as the higher ranks of the Parisian people. She was young, she was beautiful, and of spotless reputation; she had been maliciously slandered; the heir of an illustrious house had died in defence of her honour; and lastly, and above all, perhaps, she was the sister of the gallant youth who had snatched the laurels from Spain and revived the military glory of France. It was this renown which invested her name with a halo of false glory, and excited enthusiasm, particularly amongst the populace, when they welcomed her as the heroine of the Fronde.

CHAPTER XXV.

Preparations for the Public Fêtes Suspended. — A Defeat, a Victory, and a Death.— Constancy Rewarded.— The "Carte du Pays de Tendre."— Woman's Social Equality Recognized.— Rambouillet on the Wane.— Claire Angélique d'Angennes. — A Duel by Torchlight. — Salons of Madame la Princesse. — Sévigné at Rambouillet.

ANNE of Austria had intended that a series of public *fêtes* should be given in celebration of the victory of Rocroi, and in honour of the young general and the army that had won it. But so entirely had the Coligny-Longueville affair occupied the time and attention of the queen, the minister and the court, and the minds of the people, that the preparations for these national rejoicings were entirely suspended. The excitement having in some degree subsided, they were ordered to be renewed. Again, however, the festivities were deferred; for scarcely had the Duc d'Enghien received the felicitations of his friends, and the thanks of the queen, than news arrived that Turenne had been defeated at Marienthal.

With all speed the duke returned to the army, and offered battle to General Merci on the plains of Nordlingen. Fortune again favoured the

French army, and their victory was a decisive one. The distinguished Spanish commander-in-chief was killed. His conqueror buried him, with full military honours, near the battle-field, and placed on his grave a Latin inscription, signifying, "*Arrête, voyageur, tu foules un héros.*" Following up his successes, as before, the prince besieged and took Dunquerque, which then first fell into the hands of the French.

At Nordlingen the young Count de Pisani was killed,—a severe blow to the Rambouillet family, and to their circle generally. Voiture, who was deputed to compliment the duke on his victory, was utterly unable to do so from emotion, so deep was his grief for the loss of his friend,— the participator in most of his jokes and frolics, and whose regard for him was great and sincere. The *réunions* of the marquise were, of course, for some time interrupted, and, when resumed, were less frequent than before, for the loss of her son was naturally an abiding sorrow with her.

But Julie d'Angennes is at last to become Duchesse de Montausier. The duke has wooed her for full thirteen years, and youth and the best years of life are fast slipping away,—for Julie is now thirty-seven, and the duke thirty-four. It was then as unusual as now to find the amiable and attractive daughter of a rich and noble French family unmarried at that age. It has been said that the lady, before bestowing her hand, compelled her lover to pass through all the gradations of the tender passion prescribed by the code of laws that regulated the sentimental chivalry and love *à la mode* de l'Hôtel de Rambouillet, to which a sort of guide was furnished by the famous "Carte du Pays de Tendre" of Mademoiselle de Scudéry.

But this is an error. A very sincere attachment existed between the duke and Mademoiselle d'Angennes, as the constancy of both attests. The only obstacle to their marriage was the duke's Protestantism, and it was a formidable one, removed only by his abjuration. It does not appear that he was influenced by any material change in his religious convictions. Henry IV. said "a crown was worth a mass;" the Duc de Montausier thought the hand of his Julie worth no less. Doubtless both those renegades found arguments that readily silenced the scruples of conscience; for conscience is a good, easy, tractable creature until the deed that first disturbed her be done, when she often begins to fret and to sting in good earnest. As to the "Carte du Pays de Tendre," it was surreptitiously obtained, and, to the great annoyance of Mademoiselle de Scudéry, published, with the view of bringing ridicule on the *société polie* or *précieuse* of Rambouillet,—*précieuse*, a word recently invented, then signifying a person of good breeding and distinguished manners.

On this map of the progress of the tender passion was first marked the "Lake of Indifference," whence you looked on the shores of "Disinterested Pleasure," — the pleasure the mind derives from first gazing on a beautiful object, in this case, a fair lady. Thence the road was traced to the "Hamlet of Respect," and onwards to the villages of "Billet-doux," "Billet galant," "Jolis Vers," "Complaisance," "Soumission," "Petits Soins," "Assiduité," till you came to the larger villages or small towns of "Empressement" and "Sensibilité," leading direct to the city of "Tendre," on the "River of Inclination," which flowed into the "Mer Dangereuse." There, after tossing about, "from the base of the wave to the billow's crown," if you did not get wrecked, or founder in a storm, you had a chance of finding at last the "Haven of Rest," which, of course, meant marriage. It was silly, no doubt; but it was intended merely as part of an evening's amusement for five or six friends. It was quite in harmony with the overstrained chivalric notions that found favour at Rambouillet, and which were encouraged with the object of suppressing the shameless depravity so long sanctioned by the example of the Valois and of Henry IV., and to introduce respect for woman and purity of life. The Hôtel de Rambouillet and its stately hostess deserve to be celebrated; for it was in the famous *salon bleu* that the pleasures of social intercourse were first realized in France, and learning and mental gifts met with their due appreciation. There, too, the French first recognized the social equality of woman, while the blameless life of the marquise set an example to her sex, which, if all her society did not follow, all were there compelled, by putting on the semblance of doing so, to honour. For accomplishing so much in the midst of depravity and a demoralized court, the few affectations of the Rambouillet circle may be pardoned.

Amongst the *beau monde* of the Marais there was decidedly more sociability after the death of Richelieu. Other *salons* were then opened in the hôtels of the *noblesse* for the reception of "*la société polie;*" and subsequent to Nordlingen, both Rambouillet and its marquise were considered to be on the wane. When Julie became Duchesse de Montausier, though she and the duke resided at the Hôtel for two years after their marriage, yet the *habitués* of the *salon bleu* dropped off by degrees; not from its loss of *prestige*, but because the receptions were but occasional, and had then to be announced. The marquise, too, began to lose her love of being always surrounded by a brilliant throng of the stars of the *beau monde* and the *élite* of the world of literature. She had lost both her sons; Julie, one of the great attractions of the Hôtel, would soon be leaving her; and the Marquis de Rambouillet, who for years had been constantly employed in foreign missions, had lately returned home in failing health. There, however, remained yet an unmarried daughter, Claire Angélique, the youngest of the family, and for the sake of this lively coquette, who eventually became the first wife of the Comte de Grignan — afterwards the son-in-law of Madame de Sévigné — the *salon bleu* was not yet finally closed.

This sprightly young lady — whose wit and beauty are celebrated by Madéleine de Scudéry in her great romance of "Le Grand Cyrus" * — was a very fascinating flirt, with a brilliant complexion and magnificent eyes. She had none of the staidness and reserve of Julie, and was introduced into the Rambouillet circle only when its influence, from the less frequency of its *réunions*, was on the decline, Claire being many years younger than her sister. Full of gaiety, yet capricious and imaginative, "it was difficult to please her," says her friend Madéleine. She found the "*société polie et littéraire*" prudish, stilted, wearisome, and complained of it so naïvely, so charmingly, that while all who heard the story of her *griefs* were amused, all sympathized with and admired her. Until she married M. de

---

* Vol. vii., p. 264. Julie and her sister are there described under the names of Philonide and Anacrise. The character also of the Duc de Montausier is given under the name of Mégabates.

Grignan,—whose third wife, also a difficult lady to please, to describe his ugliness, borrowed Guilléraguc's *mot* on Paul Pélisson: *Qu'il abusait du privilége qu'ont les hommes d'esprit d'être laid*," —Mademoiselle Claire appears to have been willing to receive admiration from whatever quarter it came.

Voiture, whose wit and lively sallies pleased her, fought a duel on her account with the Intendant of Madame de Rambouillet, a Monsieur Chaventré. He, as well as Voiture—though neither had any serious intentions—"paid homage" to the younger Mademoiselle d'Angennes. Voiture thought this presumption, and did not choose to allow it; he therefore sought a quarrel with his rival, and a duel was the result. It was fought at midnight,—the combatants being lighted by torches,—and Voiture was wounded in the thigh. He wrote an account of it to his friend the Comte d'Avaux, and confessed that he was rather ashamed of himself.

But Voiture was always ready with his sword, as was the fashion of the day. While at Brussels, on some business connected with the affairs of the Duc d'Orléans, he fought a duel by moonlight with a Spaniard with whom he had been gambling, and suspected of cheating him. He was constant to the end in his attachment to the scene of his regeneration; but he was often away from the capital, engaged in diplomacy, and other uncongenial business of the state incidental to the places of trust and honour thrust upon him. Georges and Mademoiselle Scudéry were gone to Marseilles, and the *salons* of Madame la Princesse were thronged since the brilliant military exploits of her son and the triumph of her daughter. The appointment of the prince to be president of the queen regent's council had also given influence and power to the Condé family, as one of the channels through which places and pensions were to be obtained. The princess was, therefore, more frequently seen in her own *salon* or at the Palais Royal — before or after "*le petit conseil*" — than, as formerly, in the *salons* of Rambouillet.

The marquise, however, continued occasionally to receive a distinguished circle for three or four years longer, and it is probable that Madame de Sévigné, who was married in 1644, may have sometimes been present at those *réunions*, which then so rarely took place, but for which invitations were on that account the more eagerly sought. Somaize has included Madame de Sévigné's name in his "Dictionnaire des Précieuses;" her connection with Rambouillet was, however, of the slightest. The famous Hôtel would seem to have accomplished its mission, and virtually to have ended its career with the marriage of Julie d'Angennes.

CHAPTER XXVI.

Victories of the Duc d'Enghien. — The Court Envious and Alarmed. — "Veni, Vidi, Vici." — The Duchess received by Turenne. — Her Conquests at Münster. — Death of Monsieur le Prince. — His Splendid Funeral. — Italian Opera Introduced. — The Queen's Piety Vexes Mazarin. — Mademoiselle de Montpensier. — Louis XIV. and Prince Charles. — The Rival Beauties Reappear. — La Belle des Belles Triumphant.

MAZARIN and his adherents had begun to look with jealous eyes on the ascendency acquired by the Condé family in the councils of the state and in the esteem of the people. No name was so exalted as that of the Duc d'Enghien. His brilliant victories, — due no less to ardour, that inspired his troops with courage, daring as his own, that quailed before no dangers or difficulties, than to able generalship, — excited the enthusiasm of the nation. The Duchesse de Longueville, whose influence was paramount in her own family, had her part also in the homage publicly paid to her distinguished brother. "A friendly word, or a smile of approval, from the *belle duchesse*, was coveted as if some sovereign good would result from it," and no sort of court favour, or gift of fortune, appeared to be valued unless it came from a member of the Bourbon-Condé family; in whom all the grandeur, the glory and the gallantry of the period then concentred.

It seemed time to withdraw the young hero from the scene of his victories; for Mazarin having imbued the weak mind of the queen with his own vague suspicions and fears, the court felt a secret alarm; bore uneasily the grand airs of Madame la Princesse, and looked with envious eye on the social preëminence to which public opinion had raised the Duchesse de Longueville. A detachment of raw troops — ill-equipped and ill-paid — was hastily assembled, and D'Enghien recalled from Flanders to take the command and proceed to Catalonia. He besieged Lerida, but without success. In his absence, the troops of the empire grew bolder. The Archduke Ferdinand threatened Artois and Lens, and it became necessary to summon back the hero of France with all speed.

Demonstrations of enthusiastic joy welcomed him when he rejoined his army. His comrades-in-arms, who had been victorious under his leadership, hailed his return with delight, and like the renowned hero of antiquity, young Louis de Bourbon "came, saw, and conquered." His battle-cry was "*Amis! souvenez-vous de Rocroi, Fribourg et Nordlingen!*" and Lens was added to the number of his victories. The archduke barely escaped being made prisoner. The Imperialists and Spaniards who composed his army fled in disorder. Five thousand prisoners, numerous standards, many field-pieces, and the battle-plain strewn with the dead, attested the decisive nature of the victory. Gaston d'Orléans, meanwhile, had taken Gravelines; and Turenne, Landau.

Peace became possible, and the Duc de Longueville, with the Comte d'Avaux, was named to attend the congress of ministers. The duke lingered awhile in Paris,— he waited for his duchess, whose head was a little turned by the successes of her brother, and the adulation of her train of humble adorers. She was immersed, too, in the pleasures which the wild joy of the Parisians had led them to indulge in, notwithstanding the frightful distress that prevailed. But peace, peace would rectify all. The duke, urged to proceed to his post, set out alone. After a short interval, the duchess, accompanied by her step-daughter, followed her husband, who at last seems to have fallen in with the general opinion that Madame de Longueville was to be set on a pedestal and worshipped.

They were attended by a numerous escort of cavalry, commanded by le Comte de Martigny, Lieutenant des Gardes, and the duke came as far as Wesel to meet the duchess and his daughter. Turenne then commanded on the Rhine. To do honour to the "*belle des belles*," he received her with his army ranged in order of battle, and, to gratify her, the troops manœuvred before her. Turenne had the reputation of being "*très sensible à la beauté*," as well as an able general, and the beauty of the duchess did not fail to make a deep impression upon him. He had not seen her since she had had the small-pox, and the only difference he finds in her, as he says in his letters to his sister, is that "she is more lovely than ever," — "*d'une beauté surprenante.*"

At Münster she was received with honours that might have gratified the hero of Rocroi and Lens himself. Infantry, cavalry, flags, and banners, with all the military and diplomatic grandees assembled there, were waiting her arrival. It was a triumphal entry, and there was in her train no more humble follower than her husband. The scales had fallen from his eyes, and he wondered at the blindness that had made him a worshipper of the mature charms of Madame de Montbazon and insensible to those of the youthful divinity he now adored in his wife. Terrible havoc her beauty made of the hearts of the wily diplomatists. It is wonderful, rivals as they were for her smiles, that they ever agreed on that Peace of Münster. They were certainly a long time about it, and probably the distracting beauty of Madame de Longueville was the cause.

The Comte d'Avaux, Voiture's friend, and a *bel-esprit* of some note, as well as a clever diplomatist, was quite enslaved by her charms. His

Prince de Condé (le grand Condé)

letters to Voiture were filled with her praises and accounts of the sensation everywhere caused by her beauty. Her life at Münster was but a succession of triumphs, and, from D'Avaux's reports, she enjoyed them immensely. Her portrait was taken by Anselme Vanholl, and was engraved, together with those of the duke, and the Comtes d'Avaux and Servien. They formed part of the collection of portraits of princes and diplomatists assembled at Münster to discuss the terms of peace. It is not the most pleasing of the few portraits still extant of *la belle duchesse.* It has an expression of weariness and languor. Probably it was the expression of her feeling at the time, for she had begun to weary of Münster and to sigh for Paris. Friends were constantly urging her to return. Voiture, who wrote often, told her that " Rambouillet was longing for the sunshine of her presence, and that *" toutes les ruelles gémissaient de son absence."*

While she was at Münster her father died, and the Duc d'Enghien, become Monsieur le Prince, was henceforth generally known as *" le Grande Condé."* He is described by Voltaire as a man of spirit and probity, when probity was more the exception than the rule amongst members of the government. His household, he says, offered an example of economical management that Mazarin would have done well to imitate in regulating the expenditure of the state. Those, however, who were contemporaries of Monsieur le Prince speak very differently of him. He was immensely wealthy, yet extremely avaricious. Madame de Motteville says, "*Il était sale, vilain avare.*" Tallemant confirms her opinion, in even stronger terms. The queen paid a visit, on the occasion, to the princesse, "*mais plutôt pour se réjouir avec elle que pour la plaindre.*" Madame de Rambouillet, on hearing of his death, remarked that "the day he married the princess, and conferred such high rank upon her, and the day of his death, when he restored her to liberty and left her a large fortune, were the only days of her life with him on which she could be congratulated."

The funeral of the prince was of extraordinary splendour, which gave occasion to much irreverent joking and raillery. It was said, "Surely, the soul of one who had been so excessively penurious and grasping in this world, must be suffering agony in another, if aware of the sum uselessly wasted by the princess on his worthless body."

To amuse the queen and dispel the gloom that had crept over the court, — for both Anne and her minister were daily becoming more unpopular, — Mazarin introduced opera, and sent to Italy for singers. An opera by Giulio, entitled "La Festa théatrale della Finza Pazza," had been given in the previous year — 1645 — at the Petit

Luxembourg. Saint Évremond called it "a fantastic production of poetry and music." He disapproved of it entirely. He says: "A play sung from the beginning to the end, as if the persons represented had come to the absurd understanding of discoursing in music on the most commonplace, as well as most important, concerns of life, is contrary to nature; it wounds the imagination, and offends the understanding." "*L'esprit ne pouvant concevoir un héros qui chante s'attache à celui qui fait chanter; et on ne songe guère à Thesée ni à Cadmus.*"

Mazarin's first attempt to popularize these "*Comédies en Musique, avec machines à la mode d'Italie*," was not successful. It took place in the small *salon* of the Palais Royal, and greatly wearied the select audience of about thirty persons invited to see it. But on the Shrove Tuesday following, he gave the court an entertainment of the same kind on a larger scale. A Signora Leonora came from Rome to sing the chief part (the opera was "Orphée"), and Signor Forelli, a famous machinist, to arrange and manage the changes of scenery *(changements de perspectives)*. The costumes are described as rich and elegant. But the piece lasted six hours, and though the change of scenery surprised and delighted, and, from complaisance, all professed to admire, "*on pensait mourir d'ennui.*"

Three times a week and for two successive

months this opera was given in the theatre of the Palais Royal; and the queen, fearing to displease the cardinal, underwent the infliction of being always present at its representation, from the first scene to the last. On one occasion, when the opera was so timed that it interfered with her devotions, she left about the middle of the piece. Mazarin took great offence at this, and was further annoyed, almost to the extent of withholding forgiveness, by her refusal to allow the opera to be played in Lent. The extreme vexation he displayed greatly amused the court. To see him mortified afforded the keenest delight to his enemies, and this insignificant matter, in which the queen had ventured, at the risk of incurring the cardinal's displeasure, to have her own way, became the subject of many a lively jest at his expense, and caused many a laugh in the *salons*.

After the first representation of "Orphée" on the afternoon of the Mardi-gras, a ball was given by the queen. Mademoiselle de Montpensier then made her *début*, wearing the crown jewels, with which the queen with her own fair hands had adorned her. Mademoiselle was then in her twentieth year, and, we are told, "*d' une beauté remarquable.*" She was tall, her figure elegant, her complexion fair, and she had fine eyes and a very pretty mouth. She was lively and witty, and her sallies were often keen and cutting. She was of a hasty temperament, and liable to be carried away by her feelings, which was unfavourable to her complexion; for with every passing emotion the eloquent blood rose and suffused her fair face. Mademoiselle was not wanting in generous impulses, but she was troubled with a most impetuous temper.

On the occasion referred to she was resplendent with diamonds and pearls, scattered over her dress and her hair, and adorning her fair arms and throat. They were attached by narrow ribands — white, crimson, and black -- to her dress of white taffetas and lace. They glittered, too, in the bouquet of flowers she wore — her elaborate coiffure being completed by three feathers of the colours of the ribands, drooping gracefully on her neck.

The little king, then in his ninth year, was present at this ball, as was also Charles, Prince of Wales; for the troubles in England had compelled Queen Henrietta to seek refuge in France. Louis XIV. was not a handsome child. He had just recovered from the small-pox, and was very perceptibly marked with it. His complexion was dark; he was small for his age, but fat and thickset. His features were not prominent, and he had the ugly Gascon-Bourbon nose of Henry IV., but not the hooked chin which gave that jovial monarch so comical an expression. His eyes were large and nearly black, his eyebrows strongly marked, and his countenance was rather grave for his years. Already he gave himself very grand airs, and seemed well to have learned the lesson — almost the only one he readily imbibed or that was diligently taught him — that he was not of the same clay that ordinary humanity is made of.

Louis was dressed in a tunic of black satin, embroidered in gold and silver; long crimson silk stockings and black shoes with crimson rosettes, deep lace on the ends of his short, loose, satin drawers, and crimson feathers in his hat. Young Charles was similarly dressed. He is described as being very dark, with large black eyes; intelligent in appearance, and very lively. He interested the company greatly.

Madame de Montbazon — who had partly recovered the queen's favour and some portion of her lost *prestige* — appeared at this ball in a dress elaborately embroidered in seed-pearls. She was in high beauty that night, in spite of the *terrible quarantaine*, then, *bien sonnée;* but a fine autumn is not unfrequently more beautiful than summer. Her rival, she heard with vexation, was about to reappear in the *beau monde* of Paris, to shine there with greater *éclat* than before; as the duchess was declared, by her admirers, to be more beautiful and *spirituelle* than ever. She had seen the world; she had acquired more ease of manner, and, in a word, was, so they said, "truly a model of perfection."

Mazarin got up an opera especially for her gratification; he flattered and courted all who were favoured with her esteem and regard; and to gain her favour was to become the favourite of fortune. In her *ruelle* all the intrigues against the court were carried on, and gradually she was induced to interfere in those political troubles and dissensions which filled the country with discord, and which, with a little more firmness and energy, on the part of the chiefs of the rebellion that ensued, would probably have produced similar results in France to those of the revolution in England.

END OF VOL. I.

www.ingramcontent.com/pod-product-compliance
Lightning Source LLC
Chambersburg PA
CBHW021240240426
43673CB00057B/906